IMPACT

CALIFORNIA SOCIAL STUDIES

People
Who Make a Difference

INQUIRY JOURNAL

McGraw Hill

Program Authors

James Banks, Ph.D.
Kerry and Linda Killinger Endowed Chair
in Diversity Studies
Director, Center for Multicultural Education
University of Washington
Seattle, Washington

Kevin P. Colleary, Ed.D.
Curriculum and Teaching Department
Graduate School of Education
Fordham University
New York, New York

William Deverell, Ph.D.
Director of the Huntington-USC Institute
on California and the West
Professor of History, University of Southern California
Los Angeles, California

Daniel Lewis, Ph.D.
Dibner Senior Curator
The Huntington Library
Los Angeles, California

Elizabeth Logan Ph.D., J.D.
Associate Director of the Huntington-USC Institute
on California and the West
Los Angeles, California

Walter C. Parker, Ph.D.
Professor of Social Studies Education
Adjunct Professor of Political Science
University of Washington
Seattle, Washington

Emily M. Schell, Ed.D.
Professor, Teacher Education
San Diego State University
San Diego, California

mheducation.com/prek-12

Copyright © 2019 McGraw-Hill Education

Send all inquiries to:
McGraw-Hill Education
120 S. Riverside Plaza, Suite 1200
Chicago, IL 60606

ISBN: 978-0-07-899394-7
MHID: 0-07-899394-6

Printed in the United States of America.

9 10 11 12 13 WEB 25 24 23 22 21

Letter from the Authors

Dear Second Grade Social Studies Detective,

Who makes a difference in your life? Who made a difference in the past? Heroic people are all around us. **You** can even be a hero! In this book, you will find out about people who make a difference. You will also learn more about people's lives in our state long ago and today. As you read, be an investigator. What do you wonder about? Write your own questions and read closely to find the answers. What interests and excites you? Take notes about it. Use your notes to do a project to share what you've learned. Take a closer look at photos of real people and places. Use maps to find your way!

Enjoy your investigation into the amazing word of social studies—a world full of people who make a difference!

Sincerely,

The IMPACT Social Studies Program Authors

Orville and Wilbur Wright were known around the world as heroes of aviation. In this photo from 1909, they fly their plane in France.

Contents

Reference Sources

Chapter 1

Families Today and Long Ago

Why Is it Important to Study the History of Families and Learn About the Past?

People, Places, and Environments

How Do Maps and Globes Help Us Understand Our World?

McGraw-Hill Education

Chapter 3

Economics: Goods and Service

How Do We Get What We Want and Need?

Explore the **Essential Question**

McGraw-Hill Education

How Government Works

EQ **Why Do We Need Government?**

Explore the **Essential Question**

McGraw-Hill Education

Chapter 5

People Who Made a Difference

How Can People Make A Difference In Our World?

Skills and Features

My Notes

Getting Started

You have two social studies books that you will use together to explore and analyze important Social Studies issues.

The Inquiry Journal

The Inquiry Journal is your reporter's notebook where you will ask questions, analyze sources, and record information.

The Research Companion

The Research Companion is where you'll read nonfiction and literature selections, examine primary source materials, and look for answers to your questions.

Every Chapter

Chapter opener pages help you see the big picture. Each chapter begins with an **Essential Question**. This **EQ** guides research and inquiry.

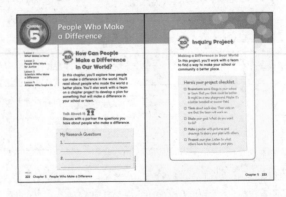

In the **Research Companion**, you'll explore the EQ through words and photographs.

In the **Inquiry Journal**, you'll talk about the EQ and find out about the EQ Inquiry Project for the chapter.

Explore Words

Find out what you know about the chapter's academic vocabulary.

Connect Through Literature

Explore the chapter topic through fiction, informational text, and poetry.

People You Should Know

Learn about the lives of people who have made an impact in history.

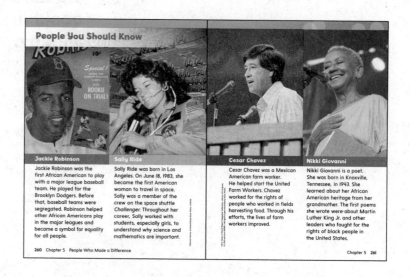

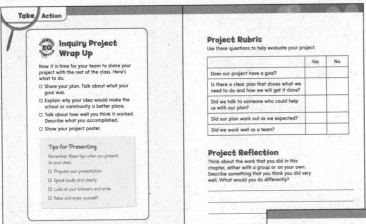

Inquiry Project Wrap Up

Now it is time for your team to share your project with the rest of the class. Here's what to do.

☐ Share your plan. Talk about what your goal was.

☐ Explain why your idea would make the school or community a better place.

☐ Talk about how well you think it worked. Describe what you accomplished.

☐ Show your project poster.

Tips for Presenting

Remember these tips when you present to your class.

☐ Prepare your presentation.

☐ Speak loudly and clearly.

☐ Look at your listeners and smile.

☐ Relax and enjoy yourself!

Project Rubric

Use these questions to help evaluate your project.

	Yes	No
Does our project have a goal?		
Is there a clear plan that shows what we need to do and how we will get it done?		
Did we talk to someone who could help us with our plan?		
Did our plan work out as we expected?		
Did we work well as a team?		

Project Reflection

Think about the work that you did in this chapter, either with a group or on your own. Describe something that you think you did very well. What would you do differently?

264 Chapter 5 People Who Make a Difference

Take Action

Present your Inquiry Project to your class and assess your work with the project rubric. Then take time to reflect on your work.

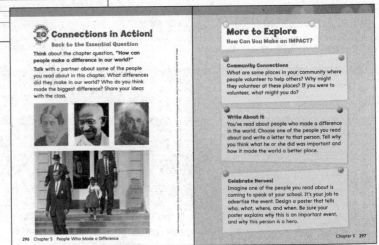

Connections in Action!
Back to the Essential Question

Think about the chapter question, **"How can people make a difference in our world?"**

Talk with a partner about some of the people you read about in this chapter. What differences did they make in our world? Who do you think made the biggest difference? Share your ideas with the class.

296 Chapter 5 People Who Made a Difference

More to Explore
How Can You Make an IMPACT?

Community Connections
What are some places in your community where people volunteer to help others? Why might they volunteer at these places? If you were to volunteer, what might you do?

Write About It
You've read about people who made a difference in the world. Choose one of the people you read about and write a letter to that person. Tell why you think what he or she did was important and how it made the world a better place.

Celebrate Heroes!
Imagine one of the people you read about is coming to speak at your school. It's your job to advertise the event. Design a poster that tells who, what, where, and when. Be sure your poster explains why this is an important event, and why this person is a hero.

Chapter 5 297

Connections in Action

Think about the people, places, and events you read about in the chapter. Talk with a partner about how this affects your understanding of the EQ.

Every Lesson

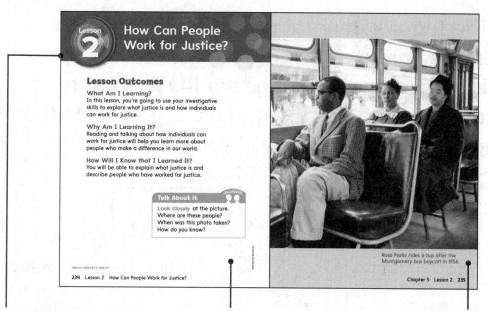

Lesson 2
How Can People Work for Justice?

Lesson Outcomes

What Am I Learning?
In this lesson, you're going to use your investigative skills to explore what justice is and how individuals can work for justice.

Why Am I Learning It?
Reading and talking about how individuals can work for justice will help you learn more about people who make a difference in our world.

How Will I Know that I Learned It?
You will be able to explain what justice is and describe people who have worked for justice.

Talk About It

Look closely at the picture. Where are these people? When was this photo taken? How do you know?

Rosa Parks rides a bus after the Montgomery bus boycott in 1956.

234 Lesson 2 How Can People Work for Justice?

Chapter 5 Lesson 2 235

Lesson Question lets you think about how the lesson connects to the chapter EQ.

Lesson Outcomes help you think about what you will be learning and how it applies to the EQ.

Images and text provide opportunities to explore the lesson topic.

Lesson 2
How Can People Work for Justice?

Martin Luther King Jr. Works for Equality

Dr. Martin Luther King Jr. was born in 1929. At the time, black people and white people were not treated the same. Many places in our country practiced segregation. **Segregate** means to keep people separate because of their race.

Dr. Martin Luther King Jr. led many marches for justice in the 1960s.

270 Lesson 2 How Can People Work for Justice?

Chapter 5 Lesson 2 271

Lesson selections help you develop a deeper understanding of the lesson topic and the EQ.

Analyze and Inquire

The **Inquiry Journal** provides the tools you need to analyze a source. You'll use those tools to investigate the texts in the **Research Companion** and use the graphic organizer in the **Inquiry Journal** to organize your findings.

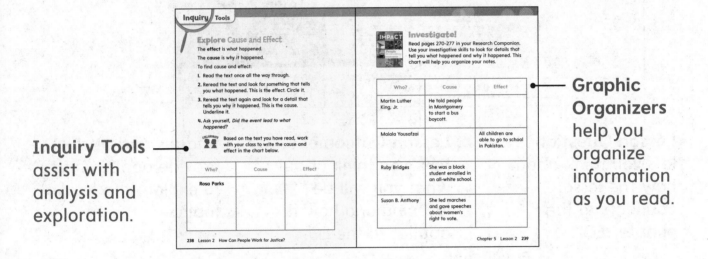

Inquiry Tools assist with analysis and exploration.

Graphic Organizers help you organize information as you read.

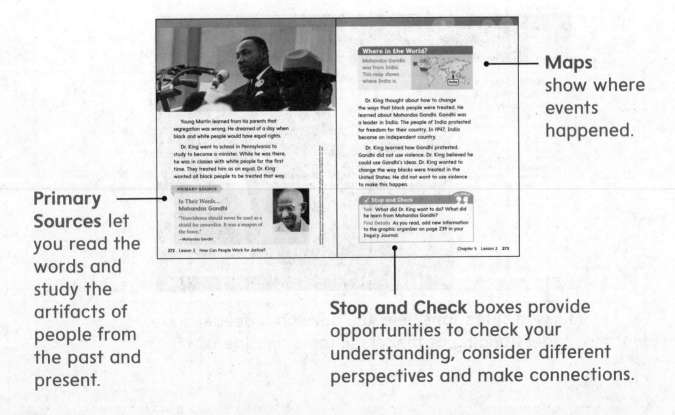

Primary Sources let you read the words and study the artifacts of people from the past and present.

Maps show where events happened.

Stop and Check boxes provide opportunities to check your understanding, consider different perspectives and make connections.

Report Your Findings

At the end of each lesson you have an opportunity in the **Inquiry Journal** to report your findings and connect back to the EQ. In the Research Companion, you'll think about the lesson focus question.

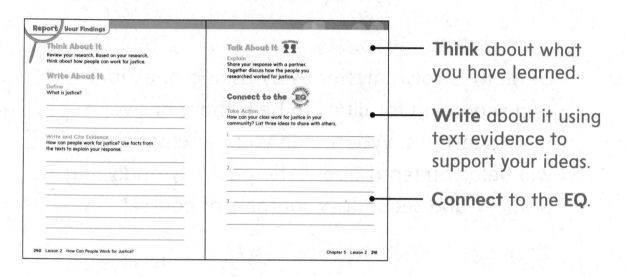

Think about what you have learned.

Write about it using text evidence to support your ideas.

Connect to the EQ.

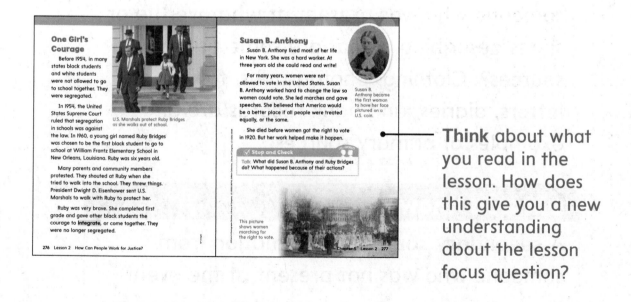

Think about what you read in the lesson. How does this give you a new understanding about the lesson focus question?

Be a Social Studies Detective

How do you learn about people, places, and events? Become a Social Studies detective!

Explore! Investigate! Report!

Investigate Primary Sources

Detectives solve mysteries by asking questions and searching for clues to help them answer their questions. Where can you get clues that will help you learn about the past? By analyzing primary and secondary sources, of course!

What are Primary Sources?

A **primary source** is a record of an event by someone who was present at whatever he or she is describing. What are some primary sources? Clothing, photographs, toys, tools, letters, diaries, and bank records are all examples of primary sources.

Did You Know?

A **secondary source** is information from someone who was not present at the event he or she is describing. Secondary sources are based on primary sources, such as a newspaper article.

Boston, Massachusetts, between 1900 and 1905

Social Studies Detective Strategies

Inspect

- Look closely at the source.
- Who or what is it?
- How would you describe it?

Find Evidence

- Where did the event take place?
- When did it happen?
- What are the most important details?

Make Connections

- Is this source like others you found?
- Are there other perspectives that you need to consider?
- What information supports your idea?

Social Studies Detectives make connections to learn about the past. Look closely at the images below. Use the Social Studies Detective Strategy to analyze the images.

Social Studies Detective Strategies
1. Inspect
2. Find Evidence
3. Make Connections

Here is another source. Ask questions and inspect the source. Look for clues to answer your questions and make connections.

September 27, 1910

Dear Diary,

I see her! I can see the Statue of Liberty from the ship! Freedom at last! Now we can own our own land. And when I'm older, I can learn at a university. But Father says that before we can live in America, we must stop at a nearby island called Ellis Island. If we fail the tests given there, we'll be sent back to Russia.

That must be why some call it the "Island of Tears."

Golda

from *"Freedom! Now What?"* by Kimberley Williams Shaw

Explore Geography

Geographers are social studies detectives who study the Earth's surface, plants, animals, and people. They use tools to help them investigate. Here are a few of the tools you need to be a geographer.

Directions

A direction is any way you can face or point. There are four main directions. They are north, south, east, and west. Directions help us answer the question, "Where is it?" Directions also help us find where something is on a map.

Globe

A globe is a special map that is shaped like a ball. It is a small model of Earth. A model is a copy of something. A globe shows what the land and water look like on Earth.

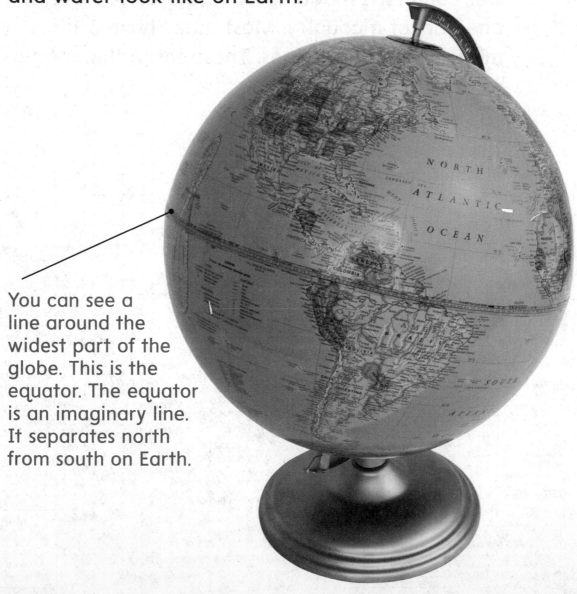

You can see a line around the widest part of the globe. This is the equator. The equator is an imaginary line. It separates north from south on Earth.

Maps

This is a map of the United States of America. The United States of America is our country. A country is a land and the people who live there. Our country is made up of 50 states. A state is one part of a country. Most maps have a title, map key, and directions. These three things help us read and use maps.

The United States of America

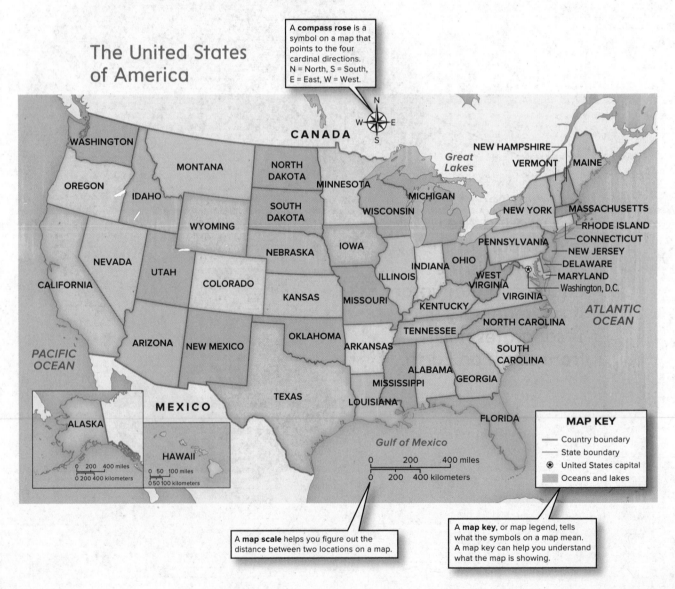

A **compass rose** is a symbol on a map that points to the four cardinal directions. N = North, S = South, E = East, W = West.

A **map scale** helps you figure out the distance between two locations on a map.

A **map key**, or map legend, tells what the symbols on a map mean. A map key can help you understand what the map is showing.

Neighborhood Maps

A map can show a large space or smaller spaces. This is a map of a neighborhood with houses, garages, driveways, and streets.

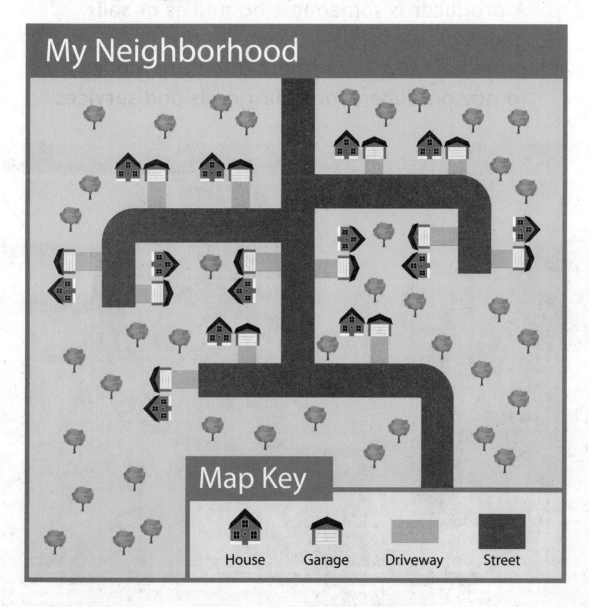

My Neighborhood

Map Key

House   Garage   Driveway   Street

Addresses

An address is a location. It tells where a house or building is located. An address has a number and a street name.

Explore Economics

A consumer is someone who buys goods or services. We are all consumers sometimes. A producer is someone who makes or sells goods or services. At times, we are all producers too. Consumers often use money to pay producers for their goods and services.

(t)StasKhom/iStock/Getty Images, (b)Ariel Skelley/Blend Images/Getty Images

This picture shows a grocery store from the early twentieth century.

Talk About It

COLLABORATE

What goods or services do you see in the picture above? Who are the consumers and who are the producers in the picture on page 16a? What details in the pictures support your ideas?

Explore Citizenship

You can make an impact by being a good citizen. The words below describe good citizens. They help us understand how to be good citizens in our home, neighborhood, school, community, country, and world.

Take Action!

You have learned to be a Social Studies Detective by investigating, finding evidence, and making connections. Then you practiced investigating geography, economics, and civics. Now it's time to explore and make an impact!

Apollo 11 astronauts plant the U.S. flag on the moon.

Be a Good Citizen

COURAGE
Being brave in the
face of difficulty

FREEDOM
Making choices
and holding beliefs
of one's own

HONESTY
Telling the truth

JUSTICE
Working toward
fair treatment
for everyone

LEADERSHIP
Showing good behavior
worth following through
example

LOYALTY
Showing support for
people and one's
country

RESPECT
Treating others as
you would like to
be treated

RESPONSIBILITY
Being worthy of trust

Chapter 1

Families Today and Long Ago

ESSENTIAL EQ QUESTION

Why is it Important to Study the History of Families and Learn About the Past?

In this chapter, you'll explore families today and long ago. You'll find out how people in the past lived. How were their lives different from yours? You'll also interview an adult to make a time line of his or her life.

Talk About It COLLABORATE

What do you wonder about how families lived in the past? Discuss your questions with a partner.

My Research Questions

1. _____

_____

2. _____

McGraw-Hill Education

HSS.2.1, HSS.2.1.1, HSS.2.1.2, HSS.2.1.3

Inquiry Project

Finding Out How People Lived in the Past

In this project, you'll work on your own to interview an adult in your family or community and make a time line of his or her life.

Here's your project checklist.

☐ **Brainstorm** some questions that you have about what life was like in the past.

☐ **Write** your questions. Be sure that people can't answer them with just a "yes" or "no."

☐ **Ask** your questions to the adult. Take notes about what he or she says. Underline big events in that person's life.

☐ **Create** a time line with the big events. Put the events in order from first to last.

Explore Words

Complete this chapter's Word Rater.
Write notes as you learn more about each word.

artifact   My Notes

☐ Know It!   _____

☐ Heard It!

☐ Don't Know It!   _____

culture   My Notes

☐ Know It!   _____

☐ Heard It!

☐ Don't Know It!   _____

history   My Notes

☐ Know It!   _____

☐ Heard It!

☐ Don't Know It!   _____

immigrant   My Notes

☐ Know It!   _____

☐ Heard It!

☐ Don't Know It!   _____

past   My Notes

☐ Know It!   _____

☐ Heard It!

☐ Don't Know It!   _____

present

☐ Know It!

☐ Heard It!

☐ Don't Know It!

My Notes

_____

_____

primary source

☐ Know It!

☐ Heard It!

☐ Don't Know It!

My Notes

_____

_____

secondary source

☐ Know It!

☐ Heard It!

☐ Don't Know It!

My Notes

_____

_____

tradition

☐ Know It!

☐ Heard It!

☐ Don't Know It!

My Notes

_____

_____

How Do We Learn About History?

Lesson Outcomes

What Am I Learning?
In this lesson, you're going to use your investigative skills to explore how we learn about history.

Why Am I Learning It?
Reading and talking about how we learn about history will help you understand how people learn about the past.

How Will I Know That I Learned It?
You will be able to talk about some of the tools people use to learn about history.

Talk About It

COLLABORATE

Look closely at the time line.
What happened first?
What happened after that?
How do you know?

HSS.2.1, HSS.2.1.1, HSS 2.1.3, HAS.CS.1

Born

First Day
of School

2010 2011 2012 2013 2014 2015

First Pet

First Sibling
Born

Look at some of
the special things
that happened in
this boy's life.

Read Look at the objects and read the text. What are the objects you see?

Circle words you don't know.

Underline clues that tell you:

- Whom did the objects belong to?

- Why are these objects important?

- What do the objects tell us about the person?

My Notes

_____

_____

_____

_____

Objects Tell Stories

The objects that people saved in the past tell us about them and the time period they lived in. These objects from the past are called **artifacts.** When we look closely at these artifacts, we can learn about a person's **history**. History is what happened in the past.

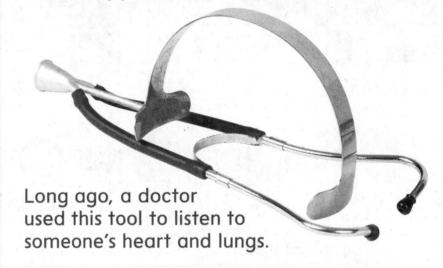

Long ago, a doctor used this tool to listen to someone's heart and lungs.

Mohair teddy bear, 1907

(t)Hemera Technologies/PhotoObjects.net/Getty Images; (b)Roland Kemp/Dorling Kindersley/Getty Images

Someone carried this watch long ago in 1912. It was owned by someone who traveled across the Atlantic Ocean. It looks different from watches we use today.

These clothes are very special. They are from a wedding.

2 Find Evidence

Reread How do the words next to the pictures help you?

Draw a box around an artifact that shows what work the person may have done.

3 Make Connections

Talk What can you tell about the person who saved these artifacts?

COLLABORATE

What different types of artifacts do you see?

Explore Key Details

A **detail** tells a piece of information.
That information can be very important to help us understand what we are learning.

To identify the key details:

1. Read the text all the way through.

2. Look carefully at the pictures.

3. Reread the text and look for the most important words. Circle those words.

4. Reread the text again and look at each picture. Draw an arrow to point to something interesting you see in part of each picture.

5. Ask yourself, *Did I find a piece of information that helps me learn more?*

 COLLABORATE Based on the text you read and the artifacts you saw, work with your class to complete the chart below.

Item	What I Learned
• Pocket watch • Tuxedo and gloves • Teddy bear • Stethoscope	

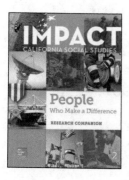

Investigate!

Read pages 12-21 in your Research Companion. Use your investigative skills to look for text evidence that tells you about tools we use to learn about history. This chart will help you organize your notes.

Item	What I Learned
Photograph	
Interview	
Museum	
Primary and secondary sources	

Think About It

Review your research. Based on the information you have gathered, how do we learn about the past?

Write About It

Define

What is history?

_____

_____

Write and Cite Evidence

What tools do people use to learn about the past? Describe one tool. Use details from the texts in your answer.

_____

_____

_____

_____

_____

Talk About It

Explain

Find a partner who chose a different tool.
Share what you wrote.

Connect to the

Take Action

Help another history detective!
Write directions for using tools to learn about history.

1. _____

_____

2. _____

_____

3. _____

_____

Inquiry Project Notes

_____

_____

_____

_____

What Makes a Family?

Lesson Outcomes

What Am I Learning?
In this lesson, you're going to use your investigative skills to explore what a family is and how families are alike and different.

Why Am I Learning It?
Reading and talking about what makes a family will help you learn more about families you know and the families of other people.

How Will I Know That I Learned It?
You will be able to explain what makes a group of people a family.

Talk About It

Look closely at the picture. What clues tell you these people could be part of a family?

HSS.2.1.1, HSS.2.1.2, HAS.CS.3

There are many kinds of families.

Analyze the Source

1 Inspect

Read Look at the title. What do you think this poem will be about?

Circle words you don't know.

Underline clues that tell you:

- Who are the people in a family?

- What do all families have?

- Where do you see families?

My Notes

_____

_____

_____

_____

_____

Families

Do all our families look alike?

No. Some are very small.

Some have grandmas in the house,

And some have none at all.

Do all our families sound alike?

No. Some are rather loud.

Some are quiet and very calm,

Just whispering's allowed.

(t)Sam Edwards/Glow Images; (b)andresr/E+/Getty Images

Do all our families look alike?

No. Some are very small.

Some have one dad, some have two,

And some have none at all.

Do all our families play alike?

No. Some ride bikes or run.

Some play games, and some jump ropes,

Or play guitars for fun.

Then how are families all alike?

What do they have lots of?

Families help, and families try.

They all have lots of love.

Monkey Business Images/Shutterstock.com

2 Find Evidence

Reread parts of the poem that are about how families are different.

Draw two lines under the words that show how families are the same.

3 Make Connections

Talk How is your family like the families in the pictures and poem?

How does your family look, sound, and play?

Explore Main Idea and Supporting Details

The **main idea** is what the text is mostly about.

The **supporting details** give examples or tell more about the main idea.

To find the main idea:

1. Read the poem all the way through.

2. Reread the text and look for what the poem is mostly about. This is the main idea.

3. Reread the text again and look for details that tell you more about that main idea.

4. Ask yourself, *Do the details explain the main idea?*

 COLLABORATE Based on the text you read, work with your class to complete the chart below.

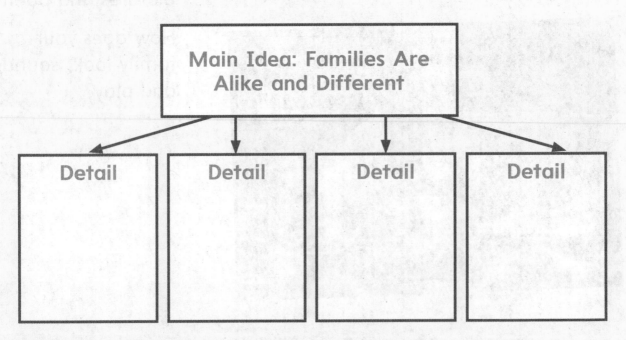

Main Idea: Families Are Alike and Different

| Detail | Detail | Detail | Detail |

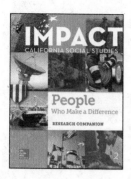

Investigate!

Read pages 22-31 in your Research Companion. Use your investigative skills to look for text evidence that tells you what makes a family. This chart will help you organize your notes.

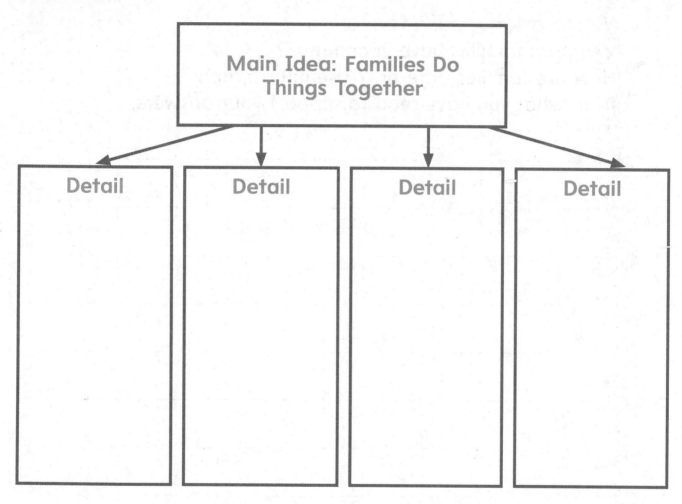

Main Idea: Families Do Things Together

| Detail | Detail | Detail | Detail |

Think About It

Based on the information you have gathered, what makes a family?

Write About It

Write and Cite Evidence

What do families have in common?
How are families different? Use information
from what you have read to support your answers.

_____

_____

_____

_____

_____

_____

_____

_____

Talk About It

Explain

Share your response with a partner.
Discuss how families are alike and different.

Connect to the

Someone asks you, "What makes a family?" Use what you've learned to write three things about most families.

1. _____

_____

2. _____

_____

3. _____

_____

Inquiry Project Notes

_____

_____

_____

_____

Lesson Outcomes

What Am I Learning?

In this lesson, you're going to use your investigative skills to learn how daily life has changed.

Why Am I Learning It?

Reading and talking about how people lived in the past will help you understand how daily life has changed.

How Will I Know That I Learned It?

You will be able to explain how the daily lives of people today are different from the lives of people in the past.

Talk About It

Look closely at the picture. What do you notice about this school? What does this school have that your school also has?

HSS.2.1.2, HAS.CS.2, HAS.CS.3

In the late 1800s, children went to a school like this one.

Analyze the Source

Schools Change

1 Inspect

Read Look at the two photographs and read the words. What do you think you will be learning about?

Circle words you don't know.

Underline clues that tell you:

- Which school is more like a school today?

- How are the two schools different?

- How are the two schools alike?

My Notes

_____

_____

_____

_____

You go to school today. One of these pictures shows a school from the present. The **present** is today or the time we are living in. Your parents, grandparents, and their parents went to school. They went to school in a time before now. They went to school in the **past**.

Some things about schools are the same. There are teachers in the present, and there were teachers in the past. Other things about schools are different. Long ago all of the students in a school studied in the same room. Today each class has its own classroom.

This a classroom from the early 1900s.

Johnston (Frances Benjamin) Collection, Library of Congress, LC-USZ62-30002

In the past, some students came to school early to help the teacher build a fire in the stove to keep the classroom warm. In the present, students may come early to work on computers.

This is a classroom today. The classroom looks different from the classrooms in the past.

2 Find Evidence

Reread How do the pictures help you see how classrooms have changed?

Draw lines to connect things that are the same in both pictures.

3 Make Connections

Write List COLLABORATE three details from the pictures that show how schools have changed over time.

ZUMA Press Inc/Alamy Stock Photo

Compare and Contrast

When you compare, you tell how things are alike.

When you contrast, you tell how things are different.

To compare and contrast:

1. Look carefully at the words and the pictures.

2. Compare them by finding things about them that are alike.

3. Contrast them by finding things about them that are different.

4. Ask yourself, *How are things different and how are they alike?*

COLLABORATE Based on what you learned about schools, work with your class to complete the chart below.

Then and Now	Alike	Different
Schools		Then:
		Now:

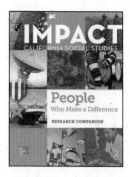

Investigate!

Read pages 32-41 in your Research Companion. Use your investigative skills to look for text evidence that tells you how things have stayed the same and what things have changed over time. This chart will help you organize your notes.

Then and Now	Alike	Different
Homes		Then:
		Now:
Work		Then:
		Now:
Clothes		Then:
		Now:
Toys and Games		Then:
		Now:

Think About It

Review your research. Based on the information you have gathered, how have the daily lives of people changed over time?

Write About It

Define
What is the past?

_____

_____

Write and Cite Evidence
Choose one part of daily life and tell how it has changed from the past. Use facts from the texts to explain your answer.

_____

_____

_____

_____

_____

_____

_____

Talk About It

Explain

Share your response with a partner. Discuss how daily life long ago is the same as and different from your daily life today.

Connect to the

History

Write a Letter

Write a letter to someone from long ago about your daily life. Based on what you have read, give at least one example to show that your daily life is different from theirs.

_____

_____

_____

_____

_____

_____

 Inquiry Project Notes

_____

_____

Why Did People Move to California?

Lesson Outcomes

What Am I Learning?

In this lesson, you're going to use your investigative skills to explore the reasons people moved to California.

Why Am I Learning It?

Reading and talking about the reasons people moved to California will help you learn more about why people move from place to place.

How Will I Know That I Learned It?

You will be able to explain several reasons that people decided to move to California.

Talk About It

COLLABORATE

Look closely at the picture. What are these people doing? When do you think this photograph was taken? How do you know?

(t)McGraw-Hill Education, (b)Ingram Publishing/SuperStock

HSS.2.1.1, HAS.CS.1, HAS.HR.1, HAS.HR.2

Millions of people came to America from other countries.

1 Inspect

Read Look at the dates. What do the dates tell you about the diary?

Circle words you don't know.

Underline clues that tell you:

- What problems did they have on the trip?

- What did they see on the trip?

- Where did the travelers spend the night on July 6?

My Notes

_____

_____

_____

On the Trail Toward California

Some people write in a diary to help them remember important things that happen. Margaret Frink and her husband followed the trail to California in 1850. They were pioneers. Pioneers are people who leave their homes and are the first to settle in a new place. This is what Margaret Frink wrote in her diary on the trip to California.

Saturday, July 6: "Part of the way I rode on horseback, the rest I walked.... After coming to the valley, we drove to the river and rested some time for dinner. In the afternoon we went seven miles further, down the valley, and encamped at sundown by a beautiful stream....*

Monday, July 8: It rained considerably during the night. Mr. Frink was on guard until two o'clock, when he returned to camp bringing the startling news, that for some unknown cause, the horses had stampeded...(the animals were found the next morning). When we arose, we found the range of mountains covered in new-fallen snow.*

This is a beautiful valley, and when under settlement and cultivation [planted with crops], will be a delightful region...."

Pioneers on the road to California, 1850

2 Find Evidence

Reread What words help you understand what "stampeded" means?

Circle how Margaret Frink thinks the valley can be improved.

3 Make Connections

Draw Sketch a picture of something that Margaret Frink described in her diary. Be sure your picture has details from the diary entry.

Explore Cause and Effect

The **effect** is what happened.

The **cause** is why it happened.

To find the cause and effect:

1. Read the text all the way through.

2. Reread the text and look for something that tells you what happened. This is the effect. Circle it.

3. Reread the text again and look for a detail that tells you why it happened. This is the cause. Underline it.

4. Ask yourself, *Did the event lead to what happened?*

COLLABORATE   Based on the text you read, work with your class to complete the chart below.

What	Cause	Effect
The horses		

Investigate!

Read pages 42-51 in your Research Companion. Use your investigative skills to look for text evidence that tells you what happened and why it happened. This chart will help you organize your notes.

What	Cause	Effect
Jobs	California had gold and other ways for people to earn money.	
Freedom	People lived in countries that were not free, and they wanted more freedom.	
Entertainment		People moved to California to be part of the entertainment industry.
Technology		People moved to California to work for technology companies.

Think About It

Think about the different reasons that caused people to move to California.

Write About It

Write and Cite Evidence

Choose one of the reasons that people moved to California. Write three sentences explaining the reason.

_____

_____

_____

_____

_____

_____

_____

_____

_____

_____

Talk About It

Explain

Work with a partner who chose a different reason than you. Share your response.

Connect to the

History

Imagine that you live someplace else and are moving to California. Write a diary entry. Explain where you are coming from and why you are moving.

_____

_____

_____

_____

_____

_____

Inquiry Project Notes

_____

_____

_____

What Would It Be Like to Move to a New Country?

Lesson Outcomes

What Am I Learning?
In this lesson, you're going to use your investigative skills to explore what it was like to come to the United States.

Why Am I Learning It?
Reading and talking about coming to the United States will help you learn about immigrants' lives.

How Will I Know That I Learned It?
You will be able to explain what you learned from reading about what it was like to move here.

Talk About It COLLABORATE

Look closely at the picture. When do you think this picture was taken?

HSS.2.1.1, HAS.CS.1, HAS.HR.1, HAS.HR.2

McGraw-Hill Education

Charles Wong, his mother, and his brother entered America through Angel Island.

Analyze the Source

1 Inspect

Read Look at the dates. What dates are on the map? Why are the dates important?

Circle names of places.

Underline clues that tell you:

- Where did the family begin their journey?

- How did they travel to the United States?

- When did they arrive in California?

My Notes

_____

_____

_____

_____

One Family's Journey

Some families left China. They wanted to find a better life for their children. This map shows the journey a family could take.

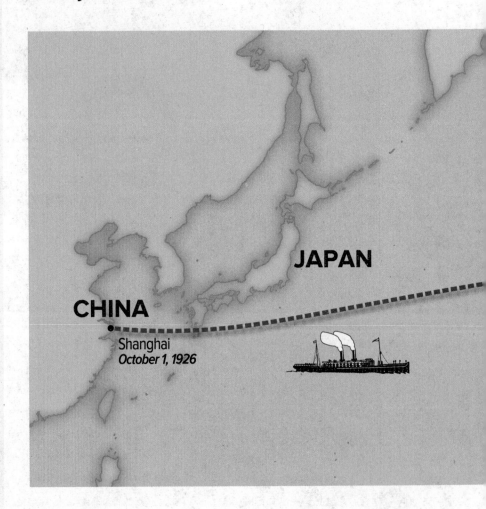

CHINA

Shanghai
October 1, 1926

JAPAN

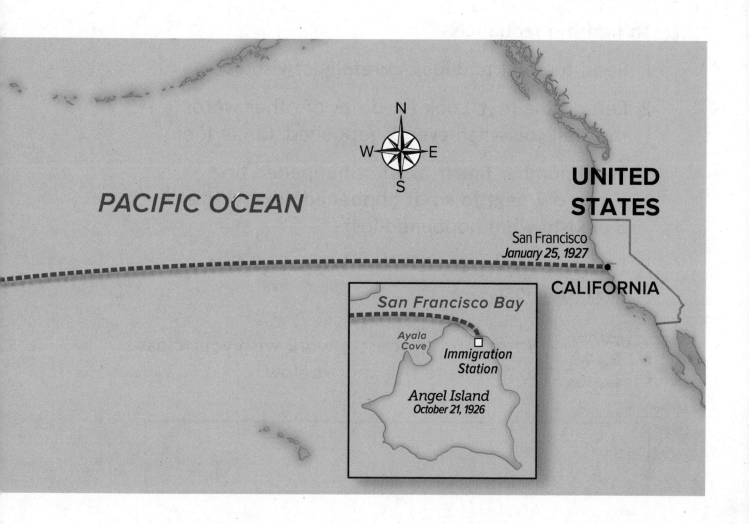

PACIFIC OCEAN

UNITED STATES

San Francisco
January 25, 1927

CALIFORNIA

San Francisco Bay

Ayala
Cove

*Immigration
Station*

*Angel Island
October 21, 1926*

2 Find Evidence

Reread Why are the dates helpful?

Number the steps of the journey, in order, on the map.

3 Make Connections

Talk What event happened first? What happened next? What happened after that?

Explore Sequence

Sequence is the order things happened.

Sequence helps you know what happened first, next, and last.

To find the sequence:

1. Read the text and look carefully at visuals.

2. Reread the text. Look for dates or other words that tell you when events happened. Circle them.

3. Put a number I next to what happened first. Write a 2 next to what happened next. Write a 3 next to what happened last.

4. In your own words, tell what happened first, next, and last.

 COLLABORATE   Based on the source, work with your class to complete the chart below.

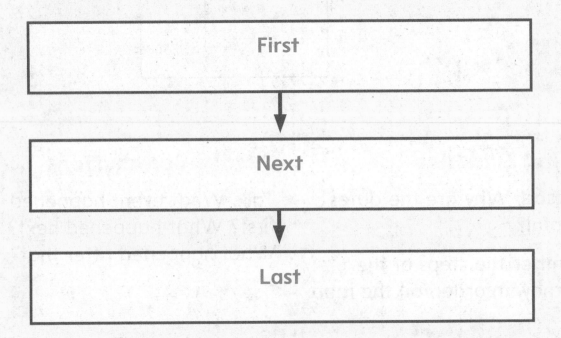

First

↓

Next

↓

Last

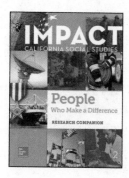

Investigate!

Read pages 52-61 in your Research Companion. Use your investigative skills to look for text evidence that tells you about what happened when families came to the United States. This chart will help you organize your notes.

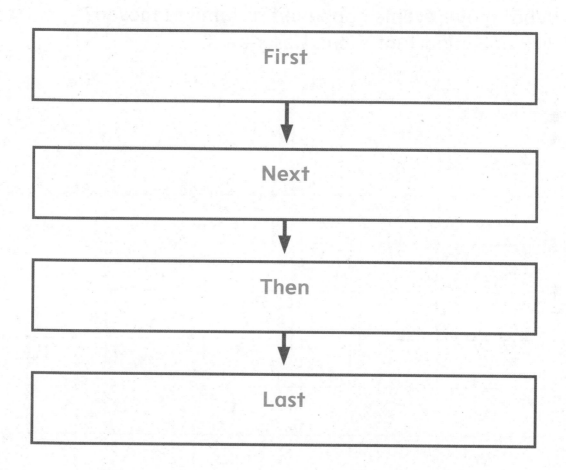

First

Next

Then

Last

Think About It

Think about families who left Asia to go to the
United States. What can you learn from their journeys?

Write About It

Write and Cite Evidence

What major events happened as families moved?
Pick one important event. Describe it.

_____

_____

_____

_____

_____

_____

_____

_____

_____

Talk About It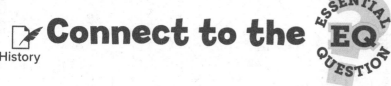

Explain

Share your response with a partner.
What events did you think were important?

Connect to the EQ ESSENTIAL QUESTION

History

Imagine that you are moving with your family to a new country. What do you think would be hard about moving? Why do you think families make that journey?

_____

_____

_____

_____

_____

ESSENTIAL EQ QUESTION   Inquiry Project Notes

_____

_____

_____

How Do People in the Past Affect Our Lives Today?

Lesson Outcomes

What Am I Learning?
In this lesson, you're going to use your investigative skills to explore how people in the past affect our lives today.

Why Am I Learning It?
Reading and talking about people from the past will help you learn why history and the efforts of people in the past are important.

How Will I Know That I Learned It?
You will be able to explain how people in the past have affected other people's lives.

Talk About It

Look closely at the words and the picture. What do you think is going on in the picture? When was the photo taken? How do you know?

McGraw-Hill Education

HSS.2.1.1, HSS.2.1.2, HAS.CS.2, HAS.CS.3

Wilbur Wright taking someone on a flight in 1910

Analyze the Source

1 Inspect

Read Look at the dates. How can you tell which event happened first?

Circle the dates.

Underline clues that tell you:

- What important thing did the Wright brothers do?

- How have airplanes changed over time?

- What do we do today that the Wright brothers made possible?

My Notes

_____

_____

_____

First in Flight

Orville and Wilbur Wright were brothers who loved to make and fix things. They saw that other people were trying to build an airplane that was safe to fly. No one could do it.

On December 14, 1903, in North Carolina, Wilbur climbed into the Wright Flyer. On the first try, it crashed. The brothers fixed the plane and tried again a few days later. This time Orville was the pilot. The plane flew for twelve seconds and went 120 feet. It was the first time humans had successfully flown an airplane!

Today, people fly short trips to visit friends or longer flights to see the world. The next time you see an airplane, think of the Wright brothers.

You may see airplanes like this today.

Michal Krakowiak/E+/Getty Images

Bessie Coleman was the first female African American pilot. She got her license to fly in 1921.

Bessie Coleman lived during a time when African American women didn't have as many rights as other people. She had big dreams for herself. When she turned 23, she moved to Chicago. She met pilots coming home from World War I. She knew what she wanted to do—fly!

Coleman worked hard and saved her money. She moved to Paris and went to pilot school. It took her seven months, but she received her pilot's license in 1921. When she returned home to the United States, many reporters came to meet her. She was the first African American woman to earn a pilot's license! She made it easier for other women and African Americans to follow their dreams.

Fotosearch/Archive Photos/Getty Images

2 Find Evidence

Reread What kind of people do you think the Wright brothers and Bessie Coleman were?

Underline one thing that happened because of the Wright brothers' first flight.

Circle the things that Bessie Coleman did in order to get her pilot's license.

3 Make Connections

Talk How have airplanes changed over time?

COLLABORATE

Explore Supporting Details

Supporting details give more information about the main idea or topic.

Supporting details help explain, describe, or give examples. To find supporting details:

1. Read the text all the way through.

2. Reread the text and identify the main idea. Underline it.

3. Reread the text and look for facts or examples that tell more about the main idea. Circle them.

4. Ask yourself, *Does each detail explain more about the main idea?*

COLLABORATE Based on the text you have read, work with your class to complete the diagram below.

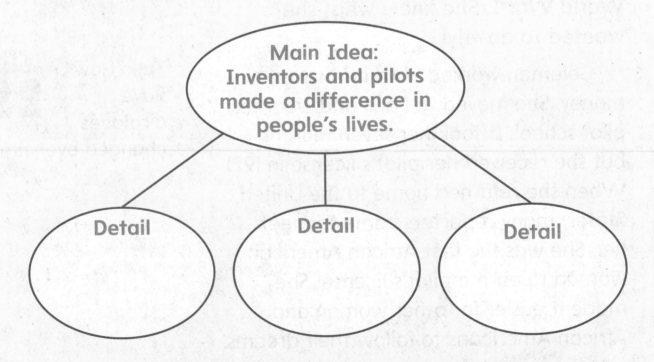

Main Idea: Inventors and pilots made a difference in people's lives.

Detail

Detail

Detail

Investigate!

Read pages 62-69 in your Research Companion. Use your investigative skills to look for text evidence that tells you about how people from the past affect our lives today. This chart will help you organize your notes.

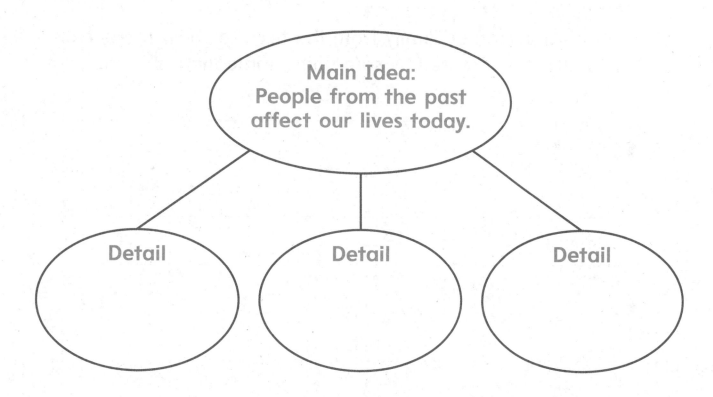

Main Idea:
People from the past affect our lives today.

Detail

Detail

Detail

Think About It

Based on what you have read, how do people
in our past affect our lives today?

Write About It

Write and Cite Evidence
Choose a person or family from the text. Tell how the person
or family was affected by something someone did in the past.

_____

_____

_____

_____

_____

_____

_____

_____

_____

Talk About It

COLLABORATE

Explain

Share your response with a partner.
What surprised you about these people?

Connect to the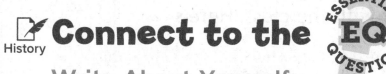

History

Write About Yourself

How do people or events from the past
affect who you are today?

_____

_____

_____

_____

_____

Inquiry Project Notes

_____

_____

_____

_____

Inquiry Project Wrap Up

Now it is time for you to complete your time line and share it with the class. Here's what to do.

☐ Get ready to speak. What events are really exciting and interesting?

☐ Show your time line to the class.

☐ Tell about the big events in the person's life. Describe them in order.

☐ Answer any questions your classmates have about the person.

Tips for Presenting

Remember these tips when you present to your class.

☐ Make your time line neat.

☐ Speak loudly and clearly.

☐ Connect with your listeners.

☐ Relax and enjoy yourself!

Project Rubric

Use these questions to help evaluate your project.

	Yes	No
Did I ask good questions?		
Did I put the events in order on the timeline?		
Were all the events on the timeline big in that person's life?		
Did my classmates understand the events?		
Did I work well on my own?		

Project Reflection

Think about the work that you did for the chapter project. Describe something that you think you did very well. What would you do differently?

_____

_____

_____

_____

People, Places, and Environments

ESSENTIAL **EQ** QUESTION

How Do Maps and Globes Help Us Understand Our World?

In this chapter, you'll explore how to use maps and globes. You'll learn about different kinds of maps, locations, and places. You'll also draw pictures of different places and write about them.

Talk About It COLLABORATE

What do you wonder about maps and how they help us to find locations? Discuss your questions with a partner.

My Research Questions

1. _____

_____

2. _____

_____

HSS.2.2, HSS.2.2.1, HSS.2.2.2,
HSS.2.2.3, HSS.2.2.4

McGraw-Hill Education

Inquiry Project

Finding Out About Different Environments

In this project, you'll be a tourist! You will make three postcards. Each postcard will have a picture of a different place. On the back of each postcard you will write about the place.

Here's your project checklist.

☐ **Brainstorm** some places you would like to visit. Then choose three of the places.

☐ **Think** about what the environment is like. Are there mountains or flat land? Are there a lot of buildings? Do a lot of people live there?

- **List** details about each place.

- **Draw** pictures on each of your postcards. Use your list of details.

- **Write** details about the place on the back of the postcard.

- **Present** your postcards to a partner. Ask questions: Are these places urban, rural, or suburban?

Explore Words

Complete this chapter's Word Rater.
Write notes as you learn more about each word.

absolute location

My Notes

☐ Know It!
☐ Heard It!
☐ Don't Know It!

_____

_____

community

My Notes

☐ Know It!
☐ Heard It!
☐ Don't Know It!

_____

_____

compass rose

My Notes

☐ Know It!
☐ Heard It!
☐ Don't Know It!

_____

_____

continent

My Notes

☐ Know It!
☐ Heard It!
☐ Don't Know It!

_____

_____

geography

My Notes

☐ Know It!
☐ Heard It!
☐ Don't Know It!

_____

_____

location

My Notes

☐ Know It!
☐ Heard It!
☐ Don't Know It!

_____

_____

relative location

My Notes

☐ Know It!
☐ Heard It!
☐ Don't Know It!

_____

_____

rural

My Notes

☐ Know It!
☐ Heard It!
☐ Don't Know It!

_____

_____

suburban

My Notes

☐ Know It!
☐ Heard It!
☐ Don't Know It!

_____

_____

urban

My Notes

☐ Know It!
☐ Heard It!
☐ Don't Know It!

_____

_____

How Do We Use Maps to Find Places?

Lesson Outcomes

What Am I Learning?
In this lesson, you are going to use your investigative skills to explore types of maps.

Why Am I Learning It?
Reading and talking about how to use maps helps you know when to use different kinds of maps.

How Will I Know That I Learned It?
You will be able to use different kinds of maps to find locations.

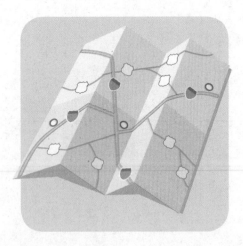

Talk About It
COLLABORATE

Look closely at the picture. Why do you think these people are using a map?

HSS.2.2.2, HSS.2.2.4

McGraw-Hill Education

This family uses a map to find where they are at Yosemite National Park.

1 Inspect

Read Look at the map title. What do you think this map shows?

Circle words you don't know.

Underline words that tell you:

- What tools are on a map?
- How do map tools help you find places?

My Notes

_____

_____

_____

_____

_____

_____

Using a Map

What do you need to know to find something in the classroom? You need to know the location. A **location** is a certain place or area where something is. In the classroom, you can find the location of a chair or a globe. Everything you see has a location. You have a location!

Maps can make it easy to see and find things. This map shows where things are in a classroom.

Maps have tools to help us read them. This map has a key. The key tells what symbols on the map stand for. On this map, an orange rectangle stands for a desk.

This map also has a special symbol called a compass rose. A **compass rose** has arrows that point to the letters N, S, E, and W. These arrows show the directions north, south, east, and west. Find the globe on the map. Now find the computer. Look at the compass rose. It shows you that the globe is east of the computer.

A map shows real places, such as the classroom.

Classroom Map

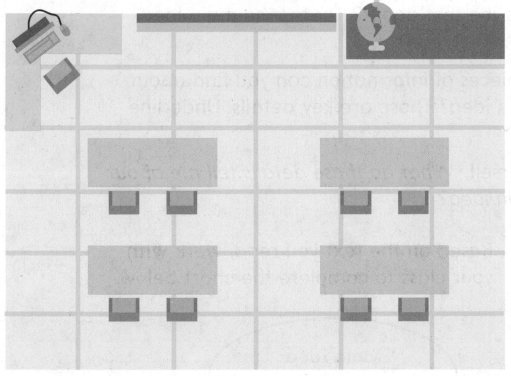

N
W   E
S

Map Key

	Globe
	White board
	Computer
	Desk

2 Find Evidence

Look Again How does the picture of the classroom help you understand the map?

Circle the map tools that help you find things on the map.

3 Make Connections

Talk Tell where you are located in your classroom.

Explore Main Idea and Key Details

The **main idea** tells what a piece of text is all about.

Key details tell more about the main idea.

To find the main idea and details:

1. Read the text all the way through.

2. What is the text about? That is the main idea. Circle it.

3. What pieces of information can you find about the main idea? Those are key details. Underline them.

4. Ask yourself, *What do these details tell me about the main idea?*

 COLLABORATE Based on the text you read, work with your class to complete the chart below.

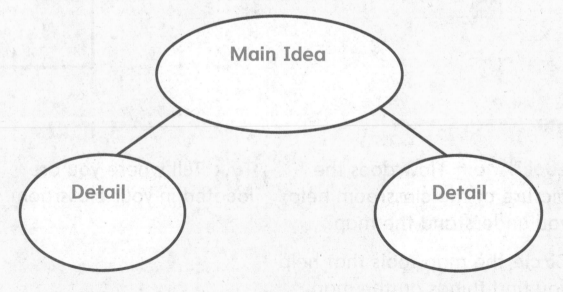

Main Idea

Detail

Detail

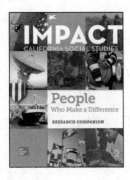

Investigate!

Read pages 80–87 in your Research Companion. Use your investigative skills to look for main ideas and details about types of maps. In each circle, show some details about maps.

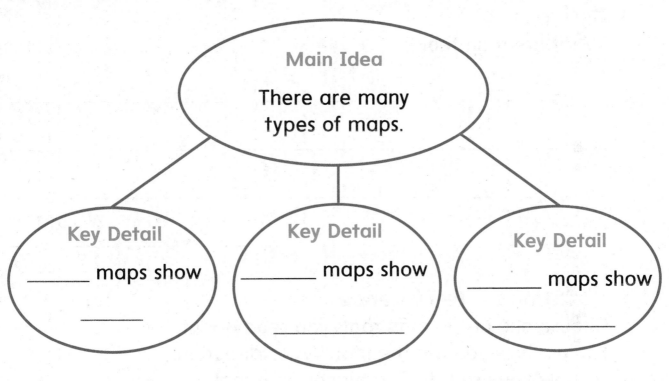

Main Idea

There are many types of maps.

Key Detail

_____ maps show

_____

Key Detail

_____ maps show

_____

Key Detail

_____ maps show

_____

Think About It

Think about your research.
What map tools do you know how to use?

Write About It

Define

What are map tools?

_____

_____

_____

Write and Cite Evidence

Choose one of the map tools you read about.
Explain how you use the tool. Write directions
on how you use it to find places on a map.

_____

_____

_____

_____

Talk About It

COLLABORATE

Explain
Find a partner who chose a different tool.
Give each other directions for using that tool.

graphy

Connect to the EQ

ESSENTIAL QUESTION

Choose a Map
Imagine you were helping your family plan a
driving trip. What kind of map would you choose? Why?

_____

_____

Imagine you wanted to find out the capital of
a country. What kind of map would you choose? Why?

_____

_____

ESSENTIAL EQ QUESTION

Inquiry Project Notes

_____

_____

_____

_____

Where Am I in the World?

Lesson Outcomes

What Am I Learning?

In this lesson, you will use your investigative skills to explore how we can describe location.

Why Am I Learning It?

Reading and talking about locations will help you describe locations.

How Will I Know That I Learned It?

You will be able to use a grid map and other tools to explain the locations of various objects and places.

Talk About It

COLLABORATE

Look closely at the picture. Why are the girl and the boy using a map?

HSS.2.2, HSS.2.2.1

A map helps us find locations.

Look Read the map title. What kinds of places do you think you will find on this map?

Circle the letters and numbers at the top, bottom, and sides of the map.

Highlight the squares where you find the:
- Soccer Field
- Barber Shop
- Movie Theater

My Notes

_____

_____

_____

_____

_____

Find Places on a Grid Map

There are different ways you can find and describe a location on a map.

The map on the next page is called a grid map. A grid map is divided by lines. The lines form squares. A letter plus a number make the name for each square.

The letters are on the left and right sides of the map. The numbers are on the top and bottom. This makes the map easier to use. To name a square in the grid map, the letter goes first and then the number.

Find the top left square on the map. It is in row A. The number at the top and bottom is I. This square is called AI. Go down three squares to find DI. The Duck Pond is in square DI.

Look for the Fire Department. What is the name of the square on the grid map?

Any kind of map can be made into a grid map. On a political map that has a grid, you can tell someone where a state is located with the name of its square. On a physical map, you can tell someone where a mountain is with the name of its square.

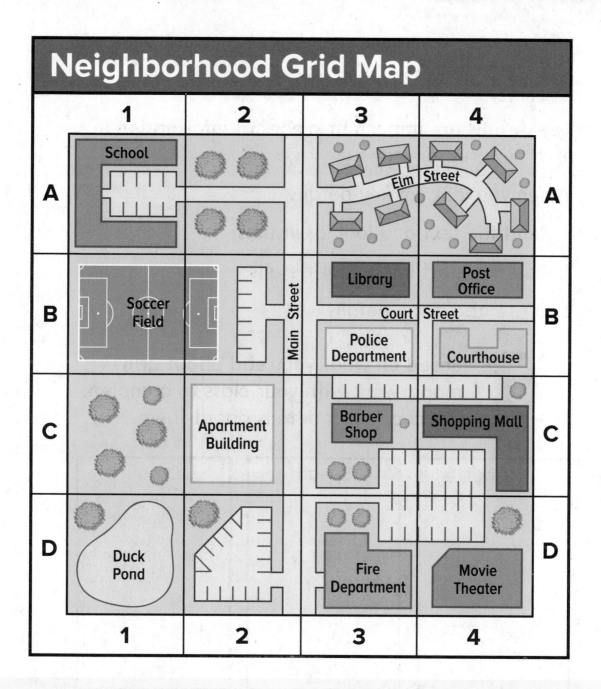

Neighborhood Grid Map

School — A1

Soccer Field — B1

Duck Pond — D1

Apartment Building — C2

Main Street

Elm Street

Library — B3

Post Office — B4

Court Street

Police Department — B3

Courthouse — B4

Barber Shop — C3

Shopping Mall — C4

Fire Department — D3

Movie Theater — D4

2 Find Evidence

Reread How do the numbers and letters on a grid map help you find places on the map?

Explain how you would find the Library on this map.

3 Make Connections

Talk How would a grid map help you find a place you want to go?

Explore Key Details

Key details are important pieces of information in text, pictures, or maps.

When you look for key details,

1. Read the text and look at visuals.

2. Find the most important details.

3. Write about the details.

COLLABORATE Based on what you read about grid maps, work with your class to complete the chart with details about them.

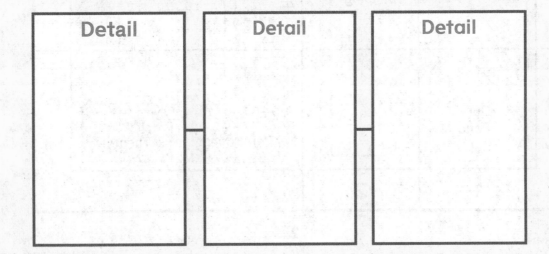

Detail	Detail	Detail

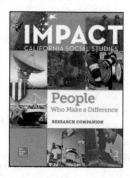

Investigate!

Read pages 88-95 in your Research Companion. Use your investigative skills to look for details about locations and how to describe them. Use this chart to help you organize your notes.

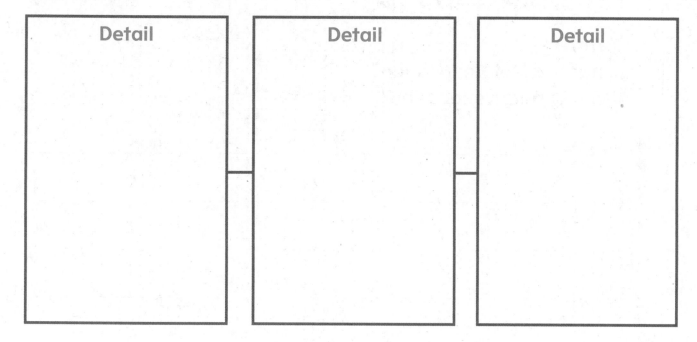

Detail	Detail	Detail

Think About It

Review your research. Based on what you read, think about how you can answer the question "Where am I in the world?"

Write About It

Define

What is absolute location?
What is relative location?

_____

_____

_____

Write and Cite Evidence

Write about California's absolute and relative location in the world.

_____

_____

_____

_____

Talk About It

Explain

Share what you wrote about California's location with a partner. Compare what you wrote.

ography

Connect to the

Write Directions

A friend wants to know how to find your school. Write some directions. Give absolute and relative locations in your directions. Make a grid map to help describe locations.

_____

_____

_____

_____

Inquiry Project Notes

_____

_____

_____

_____

Lesson 3

How Does Geography Affect the Way People Use Land?

Lesson Outcomes

What Am I Learning?

In this lesson, you are going to use your investigative skills to explore different ways people use land.

Why Am I Learning It?

Reading and talking about the land can help you understand why people live where they do.

How Will I Know That I Learned It?

You will be able to describe the communities that grow in different places.

Talk About It

Look closely at the pictures. How are the communities the same? How are they different?

HSS.2.2.1, HSS.2.2.4

76 Lesson 3 How Does Geography Affect the Way People Use Land?

You will find different kinds
of communities in California.

How We Use the Land

1 Inspect

Look Read the labels. What do the labels tell you?

Circle parts of the picture you can name.

Label the parts of the picture you circled.

My Notes

_____

_____

_____

_____

_____

_____

A **community** is a place where people live, work, learn, and have fun together. Earth's land and water can affect how and where people make communities.

There are three kinds of communities.

In **urban** communities, or cities, people live close together. There are a lot of things close by to see and do.

Urban

In **suburban** communities, people often drive to do their shopping or to go to a movie. The homes and businesses are farther apart than in cities.

Rural communities are far away from cities. There is a lot of land. People may drive to a nearby town to shop.

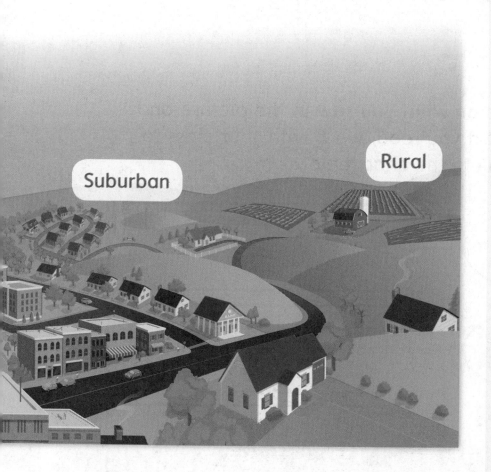

Suburban

Rural

2 Find Evidence

Look Again How are the ways people use land in urban, suburban, and rural communities alike and different?

Circle clues in the text and picture that support what you think.

3 Make Connections

Talk How are the types of communities the same? How are they different?

COLLABORATE

Inquiry Tools

Explore Cause and Effect

An **effect** is what happened.
A **cause** is why it happened.

To find cause and effect:

1. Look at the picture and read the text once all the way through.

2. Reread the text and look for something that tells you what happened. This is the effect. Circle it.

3. Find a detail that tells you why it happened. This is the cause. Draw a box around it.

4. Ask yourself, *Did the cause lead to the effect?*

 COLLABORATE

Based on what you saw in the picture and the text you read, work with your class to complete the chart below.

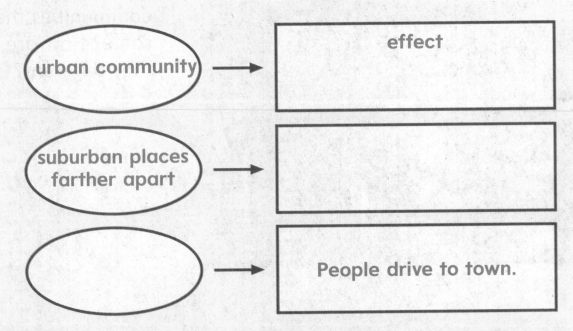

urban community ⟶ effect

suburban places farther apart ⟶

⟶ People drive to town.

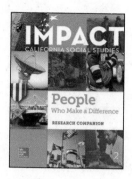

Investigate!

Read pages 96–103 in your Research Companion. Use your investigative skills to look for text evidence that tells you about the different ways that land is used in communities.

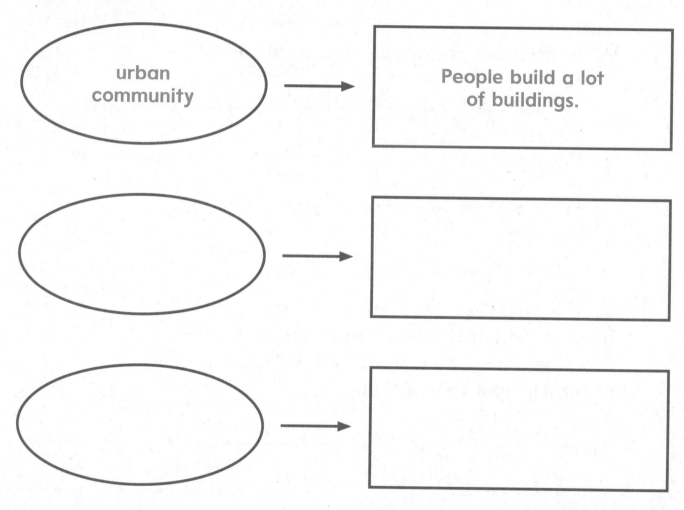

urban community → People build a lot of buildings.

Think About It

Think about your research. What did you learn about communities and their features?

Write About It

Define
What do *urban, suburban,* and *rural* mean?

_____

_____

_____

_____

Write and Cite Evidence
In what kind of community do you live? Describe it. Use the word *urban, suburban,* or *rural* in your description.

_____

_____

_____

_____

_____

Talk About It
COLLABORATE

Explain

Share your response with a partner. What details did you both use to describe your community?

ography

Connect to the EQ
ESSENTIAL EQ QUESTION

Write an Ad

What makes your community special? Why would people want to live there? Focus on the land and the features! Write an ad for your community.

_____

_____

_____

_____

_____

ESSENTIAL EQ QUESTION Inquiry Project Notes

_____

_____

_____

How Can We Describe California's Environment?

Lesson Outcomes

What Am I Learning?
In this lesson, you're going to use your investigative skills to explore California's environment.

Why Am I Learning It?
Reading and talking about California's environment can help you understand why it is special.

How Will I Know That I Learned It?
You will be able to describe features of California's environment and explain how people are working to protect it.

Talk About It

COLLABORATE

Look closely at the pictures. What can you learn about special features in California's environment?

HSS.2.2.1, HSS.2.2.4

McGraw-Hill Education

California has unique features in different areas.

(t)venonwiley/iStock/Getty Images; (b)Denise Taylor/Moment/Getty Images

1 Inspect

Read Look at the title and labels on the graphs. What do you think the graphs show?

Circle words you don't know in the text.

Underline words that tell about California's weather.

My Notes

_____

_____

_____

_____

_____

_____

Weather in California

California is a special place for many reasons. It has interesting landforms, features, and people! People like to visit California. It has great weather. California is sunny in many places most of the year.

California is not a very rainy state. Look at the graphs to see how much rain falls in two cities in California. San Diego is in the southern part of the state, and Sacramento is in the northern part of the state. Some of the rain in northern California falls as snow because the air is colder.

How are the rainfall amounts alike and different in northern and southern California?

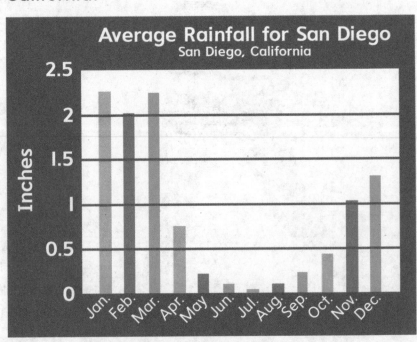

Temperature, or how hot or cold the air is, and rain are two ways that we tell about weather. We can better understand California's weather by looking at its climate. Climate is the weather in a place over a long time.

Climate affects the environment. The environment is all of the natural things that are around us on Earth. These things include land, water, air, and trees. The environment in California is special. It is different in the northern and southern parts of the state. It is different on the coast by the ocean than it is away from the ocean.

2 Find Evidence

Reread How can we describe, or tell about, the climate?

Underline clues that support what you think.

3 Make Connections

Talk What COLLABORATE did you learn about California's climate and environment? How is the climate different in northern and southern California?

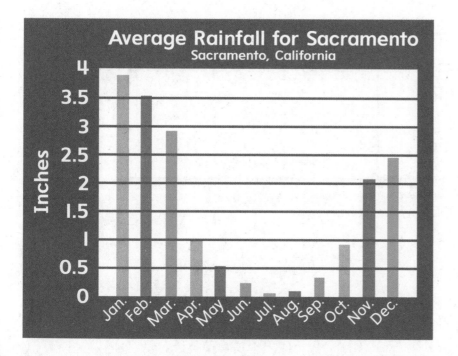

Average Rainfall for Sacramento
Sacramento, California

Explore Key Details

Key details are important pieces of information in text, pictures, and graphs.

To find key details:

1. Read the text once all the way through.

2. Look at the visuals.

3. Find the most important details.

4. Ask yourself, *What do these key details tell me about?*

 COLLABORATE Based on the text you read, work with your class to complete the chart below.

Area	What I Learned
Northern California	
Southern California	

Investigate!

Read pages 104-117 in your Research Companion. Use your investigative skills to look for text evidence that tells you about the environment in different places in California.

Area	What I Learned
Mojave Desert	
Central Valley	
Sierra Nevada	
Redwood National Forest	

Think About It

Review your research. Think about the features of California's environment.

Write About It

Define
What is an environment?

_____

_____

_____

_____

Write and Cite Evidence
Choose a feature in California.
Tell where you can find it. Describe the feature.

_____

_____

_____

_____

_____

_____

Talk About It

Explain

Share your description in a small group. What do you think makes the environment in California special?

graphy

Connect to the EQ

Write a Postcard

Imagine that you are visiting a place in California. What features does it have? What makes it special? Draw the place and write a few lines on your postcard.

Lesson 5

How Does Geography Affect the Ways People Move in California?

Lesson Outcomes

What Am I Learning?
In this lesson, you're going to use your investigative skills to explore how the features of California affect the ways that people move and travel in our state.

Why Am I Learning It?
Reading and talking about California's features will help you understand how those features affect travel.

How Will I Know That I Learned It?
You will be able to describe California's features and explain how a feature, such as mountains, affects travel.

Talk About It COLLABORATE

Look closely at the picture. How did people travel long ago? What made this form of travel useful near mountains, forests, and other features?

HSS.2.2.2, HSS.2.2.3, HSS.2.2.4

McGraw-Hill Education

Trains have moved people to and within California for a very long time.

1 Inspect

Read Look at the title and the pictures. What do you think the text is about?

Circle words you don't know in the text.

Underline words that tell about how people move in California.

My Notes

_____

_____

_____

_____

_____

_____

Moving Around in California

California has many special features, like mountains, forests, and deserts. Did you know that those features affect transportation? Transportation is the moving of people, animals, and things from one place to another.

People use many different forms of transportation.

Timothy Stubblefield/EyeEm/Getty Images

What kinds of transportation do you see in the pictures on these pages?

Long ago, people used different ways to move and get around than we use today. People found ways to make transportation better and faster. Sometimes California's special land made people have to think hard. They had to figure out how to move people over mountains, across water, up hills, and underground.

They also had to think about the kind of area. An urban area is different from a rural area. That's why an urban area might have buses or special trains to get people to work or school. In a rural area, you might need a car.

2 Find Evidence

Reread How does California's geography affect the ways people move in our state?

Underline clues in the text that support what you think.

3 Make Connections

Talk Talk about a feature in California, like a mountain. How would that affect transportation?

COLLABORATE

Explore Problem and Solution

A **problem** is something you need to think about.

A **solution** is the answer to a problem.

To find a problem and solution:

1. Read the text once all the way through.

2. Reread and look for something that tells you a question or tells you what is wrong. This is the problem. Circle it.

3. Reread the text again and look for sentences that talk about how to solve the problem. Underline them. There might be more than one way to solve a problem.

4. Ask yourself, *Does the solution solve the problem or answer the question?*

 COLLABORATE Based on the text you read, work with your class to complete the chart below.

Moving in California

↓

↓

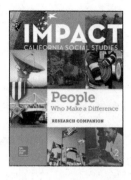

Investigate!

Read pages 118–127 in your Research Companion. Use your investigative skills to look for text evidence that tells you some steps people took to solve the problem of moving in California.

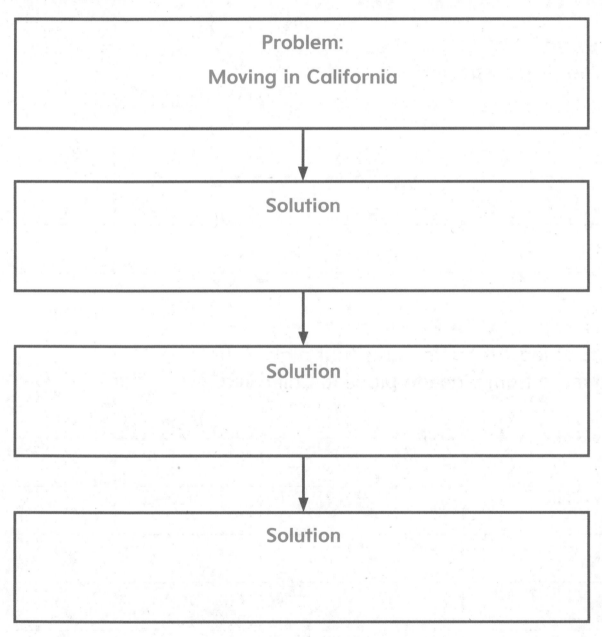

Problem:

Moving in California

Solution

Solution

Solution

Think About It

Think about your research. What features in California make it hard to move from one place to another?

Write About It

Define
What is **transportation**?

_____

_____

_____

_____

Write and Cite Evidence
List at least three features that make it hard to move from place to place in California.

_____

_____

_____

_____

_____

Talk About It

COLLABORATE

Explain

Share what you wrote with a partner.
Discuss possible solutions to problems that can make it hard to travel in California.

graphy

Connect to the  EQ

ESSENTIAL QUESTION

Plan a Trip

Look at a map of California and its landforms.
Find a place that you would like to travel.
Make a plan! What transportation would you use?
Why would you use that transportation?

_____

_____

_____

_____

_____

ESSENTIAL EQ QUESTION

Inquiry Project Notes

_____

_____

_____

Inquiry Project Wrap Up

Now is the time for you to complete your postcards and share them with a partner. Here's what to do.

☐ Look at your postcards one last time. Are there more details you want to include?

☐ Share your postcards with a partner.

☐ Read the details you wrote about each place.

☐ Ask your partner how people use each kind of land.

Tips for Sharing

Remember these tips when you share your postcards with a partner.

☐ Make your postcards neat.

☐ Speak slowly and clearly.

☐ Show one postcard at a time.

☐ Listen to what your partner says.

Project Rubric

Use these questions to help evaluate your project.

	Yes	No
Did I choose three different places?		
Did my pictures show what the land looks like?		
Did the details I wrote about each place tell how the land is used?		
Did I write about each place as if I had visited it?		
Did my pictures and details help my partner know if each place was urban, rural, or suburban?		

Project Reflection

Think about the work that you did for the chapter project. Describe something that you think you did very well. Did you choose interesting places?

_____

_____

_____

How Do We Get What We Want and Need?

In this chapter, you'll compare and contrast wants and needs. You'll learn about goods and services and how we get them. You'll also research a food item that you may have eaten. You'll find out how it got to your plate!

Talk About It COLLABORATE

What do you think is the difference between a good and a service? What about between a want and a need? Discuss these questions with a partner.

My Research Questions

1. _____

_____

2. _____

_____

McGraw-Hill Education

Inquiry Project

Finding Out Where Food Comes From

In this project, you'll research what you ate for dinner. You will draw a picture of the food you ate last night. Then you will choose one kind of food. You will find out where it came from and how it was grown or made.

Here's your project checklist.

☐ **Think** of the food that you ate for dinner last night. Draw the food on the paper plate.

☐ **Choose** one kind of food to research..

☐ **Follow** the flow chart that you worked on as a class to help you. Does the food you chose come from the same place as the one on the flow chart?

☐ **Use** good sources to research. Your teacher will help you. Make a flow chart like the one you made with the class.

☐ **Present** your flowchart to the class. Show each step. Tell where your food came from.

Complete this chapter's Word Rater.
Write notes as you learn more about each word.

consumer   My Notes

☐ Know It!   _____
☐ Heard It!   _____
☐ Don't Know It! _____

distributor   My Notes

☐ Know It!   _____
☐ Heard It!   _____
☐ Don't Know It! _____

goods   My Notes

☐ Know It!   _____
☐ Heard It!   _____
☐ Don't Know It! _____

needs   My Notes

☐ Know It!   _____
☐ Heard It!   _____
☐ Don't Know It! _____

processor   My Notes

☐ Know It!   _____
☐ Heard It!   _____
☐ Don't Know It! _____

producer

My Notes

☐ Know It!

☐ Heard It!

☐ Don't Know It!

_____

_____

scarcity

My Notes

☐ Know It!

☐ Heard It!

☐ Don't Know It!

_____

_____

services

My Notes

☐ Know It!

☐ Heard It!

☐ Don't Know It!

_____

_____

wants

My Notes

☐ Know It!

☐ Heard It!

☐ Don't Know It!

_____

_____

What Are Wants and Needs?

Lesson Outcomes

What Am I Learning?

In this lesson, you're going to use your investigative skills to explore the difference between wants and needs and why we have to make economic choices.

Why Am I Learning It?

Reading and talking about wants and needs will help you learn more about how and why people make choices.

How Will I Know that I Learned It?

You will be able to explain the difference between wants and needs. You will also be able to explain why and how people make choices.

Talk About It — COLLABORATE

Look closely at the picture. Where are these people? What does it look like they are doing?

HSS.2.4

It is shopping time.

Isadora Getty Buyou/Image Source

Analyze the Source

1 Inspect

Read Look at the shopping list. Why do you think someone made a shopping list?

Circle words you don't know.

- What types of items on the list are wants?

- What types of items on the list are needs?

- What items on the list might have to wait for another trip to the store?

My Notes

_____

_____

_____

_____

Making a List

A shopping list can help people remember what they want to buy at the store. A list may include items people need, like food. **Needs** are things people must have to live.

A list may also include items people want. **Wants** are things people would like to have but do not need. We need food to live. Ice cream is food, but it's not a need–it's a want. We need healthy food like fruits and vegetables, not unhealthy food like candy and ice cream.

Shopping list

Using a list helps us remember what to buy from the store.

When you go shopping, it can be helpful to have a list. Look at the shopping list. Circle two things that are needs. Underline one thing that is a want. People try to buy what they need first. If they are able to buy more, they might buy something they want.

2 Find Evidence

Reread How does a shopping list help?

Draw a box around each need on the shopping list.

3 Make Connections

Talk Think about the people in the photograph who are shopping. Turn back to page 107. What items might be on their shopping list?

COLLABORATE

Explore Key Details

A **detail** tells a piece of information.

That information can be very important to help us understand what we are learning.

To identify the key details:

1. Read the text all the way through.

2. Look carefully at the pictures.

3. Reread the text and look for words that tell something special about what you are reading. Circle those words.

4. Reread the text again and look at each picture. Draw an arrow to point to something interesting you see in part of each picture.

5. Ask yourself, *Did I find pieces of information that help me learn more?*

COLLABORATE   Based on the text you read, work with your class to complete the chart below.

Wants	Needs

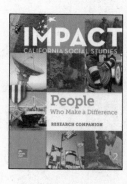

Investigate!

Read pages 138–145 in your Research Companion. Use your investigative skills to look for text evidence that tells you examples of needs and wants. This chart will help you organize your notes.

Wants	Needs
Big house, with a swimming pool	
	Shoes that protect feet

Think About It

Based on the information you learned, think about what needs and wants are.

Write About It

Define
What makes something a need?

_____

_____

_____

_____

Write and Cite Evidence
Describe why one thing is a want and one thing is a need. Cite evidence from what you've read to support your answer.

_____

_____

_____

_____

_____

Talk About It

COLLABORATE

Explain
Share your response with a partner. How can people make choices about wants and needs?

economics

Connect to the **EQ**

ESSENTIAL QUESTION

Take Action
How can you decide if something is a want or a need? Write two ways to help you decide.

1. _____

_____

_____

2. _____

_____

ESSENTIAL QUESTION EQ

Inquiry Project Notes

_____

_____

_____

_____

How Do We Use Goods and Services?

Lesson Outcomes

What Am I Learning?

In this lesson, you're going to use your investigative skills to explore the work that is done to provide the goods and services we use.

Why Am I Learning It?

Reading and talking about goods and services will help you learn more about work and economics.

How Will I Know that I Learned It?

You will be able to explain the differences between goods and services we use and workers who provide them.

Talk About It COLLABORATE

Look closely at the picture.
What job is each person doing?
How do you know?

People need different talents and skills to do different jobs.

Follow the Steps

A flow chart is a type of chart. It shows the order things happen. Look carefully at the arrows and numbers.

This flow chart shows what happens before someone buys a loaf of bread. It begins with the baker who makes the bread. What happens next? Follow the steps.

Think about the people who helped get the bread to the person who eats it. Where on the flow chart would you put the clerk who sells the bread? What other people and jobs could you add?

1 Inspect

Read Look at the title of the chart. What do you think this chart will be about?

Circle words you don't know.

Underline clues that tell you:

- Who is making something?

- What is each person doing?

- Where did the product begin?

My Notes

_____

_____

_____

_____

Bread: From Me to You

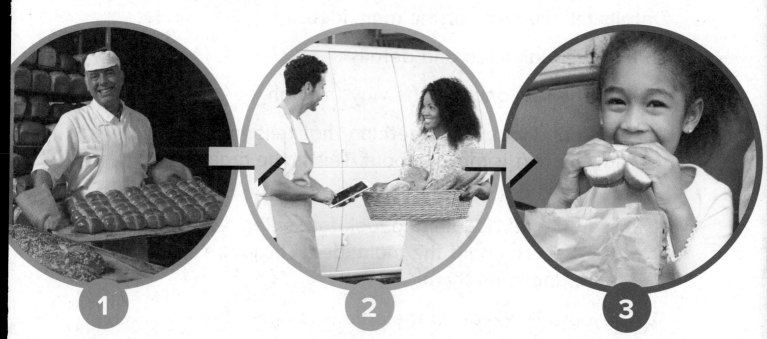

1 The baker mixes the dough and bakes the bread.

2 The driver delivers the bread to the store.

3 The person who bought the bread enjoys eating the bread.

2 Find Evidence

Reread How do the arrows help you understand the flow or order on the chart?

Circle the last step in the chart. How do you know it is the last step?

3 Make Connections

Talk Turn back to page 115. Are these people making a good or providing a service? Why do you think so?

Explore Main Idea and Details

The **main idea** tells what the text is about.

Details tell more about the main idea.

To find the main idea and details:

1. Read the text once all the way through.

2. Reread and look for something that tells you what the text is mostly about. This is the main idea. Circle it.

3. Reread the text again and look for sentences that tell more about the main idea. Those are details. Underline them.

4. Ask yourself, *What do the details tell me about the main idea?*

 COLLABORATE Based on the text and flow chart you read, work with your class to complete the chart below.

Detail	Detail	Detail

Main Idea: how bread gets to our table

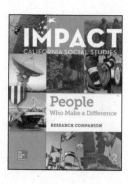

Investigate!

Read pages 146-153 in your Research Companion. Use your investigative skills to look for text evidence that tells you more about goods and services. This chart will help you organize your notes.

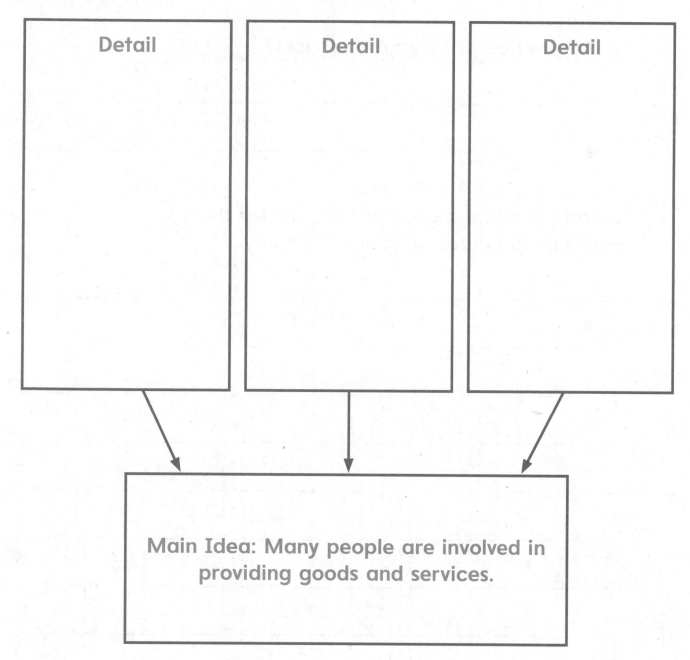

Detail	Detail	Detail

Main Idea: Many people are involved in providing goods and services.

Think About It

Review your research. What do you know about the goods and services people provide?

Write About It

Define
What are goods? What are services?

_____

_____

Write and Cite Evidence
Create an ad for a good or for a service that would be of interest to your community.

_____

_____

_____

_____

_____

_____

_____

Talk About It

COLLABORATE

Explain

Together, discuss how you use goods and services in your community.

onomics

Connect to the EQ

ESSENTIAL QUESTION

Write a paragraph that describes three of the goods and services used by your community and determine if they are wants or needs.

_____

_____

_____

_____

_____

_____

_____

_____

3

How Do Producers and Consumers Depend on One Another?

Lesson Outcomes

What Am I Learning?
In this lesson, you will use your investigative skills to explore how producers and consumers depend on each other.

Why Am I Learning It?
Reading and talking about how producers and consumers depend on each other will help you understand how our economy works.

How Will I Know that I Learned It?
You will be able to give examples of how producers and consumers depend on each other.

Talk About It

Look closely at the picture. How do buyers and sellers need each other?

(t)McGraw-Hill Education; (b)C Squared Studios/Photodisc/Getty Images

HSS.2.4.2

122 Lesson 3 How Do Producers and Consumers Depend on One Another?

Hero Images/Getty Images

Buyers and sellers need each other.

Buying and Selling

Look Look at the picture. What do you think is happening in the photograph?

Circle parts of the picture that give you clues.

Label clues that tell you:

- Who is the seller?

- What is he selling?

- Who are the buyers?

My Notes

_____

_____

_____

_____

_____

_____

When you look at a photograph, look at the whole picture first. Then look at the small details. Look at this whole photograph. Where do you think the photo was taken? What action is happening? The photograph shows what is happening at a farmers market. People are buying and selling food and handmade products.

Look at the small details in the photograph. You see some items that are for sale. At a farmers market, people sell food they have grown or items they have made. The people who grow or make things to sell are **producers**. People buy handmade items to decorate their homes or give as gifts. When people buy things they want or need, they are **consumers**.

Farmers Market

2 Find Evidence

Look Again Why is it important to look at the whole photograph as well as the small details?

Circle something that is for sale.

3 Make Connections

Talk When were you or someone in your family a consumer? Use the word *consumer* when you tell what happened. Who was the producer?

Explore Compare and Contrast

When you **compare,** you tell how things are alike or similar.

When you **contrast,** you tell how things are different.

To compare and contrast:

1. Read the text all the way through and study the photograph.

2. Reread the text and look at the pictures to find ways producers and consumers are alike. What do they have in common?

3. Reread the text again and look at the picture for ways producers and consumers are different.

4. Ask yourself, *Did I find both similarities and differences?*

COLLABORATE Based on the text you just read and what you saw in the photograph, work with your class to complete the chart below.

Consumer	Producer
wants to buy something they need or want	

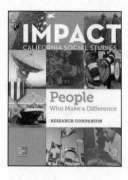

Investigate!

Read pages 154–161 in your Research Companion. Use your investigative skills to look for text evidence that tells you about producers and consumers. This chart will help you organize your notes.

Consumer	Producer
wants to get a good deal	
	buyer and seller
needs the goods the producer sells	

Think About It

Think about your research. How do producers and consumers depend on each other?

Write About It

Define

What is a producer? What is a consumer?

_____

_____

_____

Write and Cite Evidence

Choose one way that producers and consumers depend on each other. Use facts from the text to explain your response.

_____

_____

_____

_____

_____

_____

Talk About It

Explain

Share your writing with a partner. Together discuss how producers and consumers rely on each other.

nomics

Connect to the EQ

What would happen if we did not have producers? Describe how that might affect you as a consumer.

_____

_____

_____

_____

_____

_____

 Inquiry Project Notes

_____

_____

_____

Where Does the Food We Eat Come From?

Lesson Outcomes

What Am I Learning?
In this lesson, you are going to use your investigative skills to explore what is involved in producing the food we eat.

Why Am I Learning It?
Reading and talking about how the food we eat is produced will help you understand the relationship between producers and consumers.

How Will I Know that I Learned It?
You will be able to explain the steps involved in producing the food we eat.

Talk About It

COLLABORATE

Look closely at the picture. What does the picture show? What happens to the carrots after they leave the farm? How do you know?

HSS.2.4.2

Ken Welsh/Age Fotostock

It takes a lot of work and people to make a can of vegetable soup.

Read Look at the title. What do you think this poem will be about?

Circle words you don't know.

Underline clues that tell you:

- What do farmers do?

- Why does the author think that farmers are important?

My Notes

_____

_____

_____

_____

_____

A Poem of Thanks

Poems use words to create a feeling or image. Each word is carefully chosen. When studying a poem, first read the whole poem. Then go back and read each line carefully. Look for important words. Look for words that describe details.

Farmers Know
by Eva Laurinda

Through all the seasons,
throughout the land,

Farmers work with tired muscles
and care-worn hands.

Ever watchful of wind and rain,

Fire, flood, and drought,

Farmers know what their life is about:

To serve the needs and plant the seeds

That produce the food that we all need.

Working on a farm is very hard work. Farmers work long hours to harvest food that we will eat.

A farmer harvests crops.

2 Find Evidence

Reread How does the poem help you learn about the work farmers do?

Underline words that tell you why farmers are important.

3 Make Connections

Write Many people help us by growing, harvesting, and cooking our food. Write two lines of your own poem about the people who help us get food.

Explore Sequence

Sequence is the order in which things happen.

To find the sequence of events:

1. Read the text once all the way through.

2. Reread the text and look for clues about what happened first in the poem. Write a 1 by it.

3. Reread the text again and look for what happened next in the poem. Put a 2 by it. Continue through to the end.

4. Ask yourself, *Did I put the events in the correct order?*

COLLABORATE

Based on the text you read in the poem, work with your class to complete the chart.

First

↓

Next

↓

Last

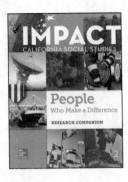

Investigate!

Read pages 162–171 in your Research Companion. Use your investigative skills to look for text evidence that tells you how we get the food we eat. This chart will help you organize your notes.

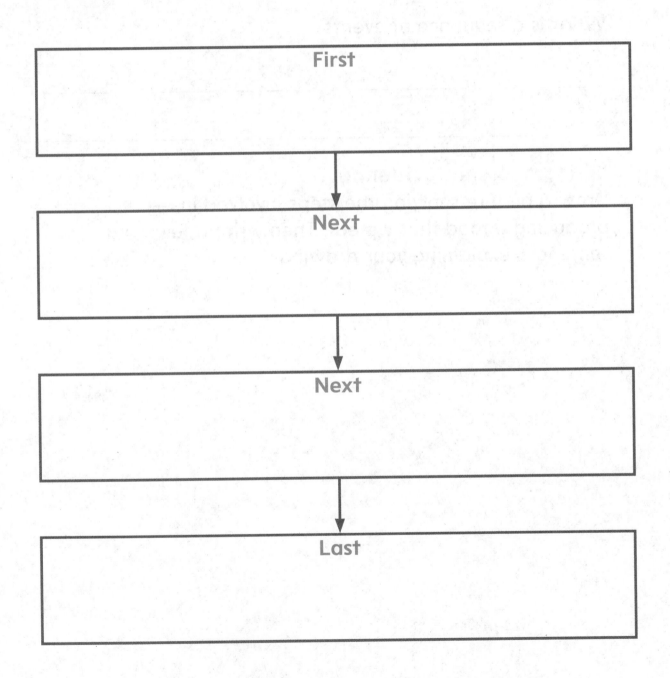

First

Next

Next

Last

Think About It

Think about your research. How does food get from a farm to your table?

Write About It

Define

What is a sequence of events?

_____

_____

Write and Cite Evidence

Draw a picture showing the steps involved in producing a food that we eat. Then write a few sentences explaining your drawing.

Talk About It

Explain

Share your response with a partner. Together discuss where food that you eat comes from.

nomics

Connect to the

List three foods that you ate today. Tell where the foods came from.

1. _____

_____

2. _____

_____

3. _____

_____

Inquiry Project Notes

_____

_____

_____

How Do Climate and Geography Affect Farming?

Lesson Outcomes

What Am I Learning?
In this lesson, you're going to use your investigative skills to explore how farming is affected by geography and climate.

Why Am I Learning It?
Reading and talking about climate and geography will help you understand why we have certain choices in the foods we get from farmers.

How Will I Know that I Learned It?
You will be able to give examples of how climate and geography affect farming.

Talk About It
COLLABORATE

Look closely at the pictures. What do you see in each picture?

HSS.2.4.3

McGraw-Hill Education

1 Inspect

Read Look at the title of the map. What do you think this map will be about?

Circle words you don't know.

Underline clues that tell you:

- What climate zone is closest to where you live?

- Why does the map have different colors?

- Why does the map need a map key, or legend?

My Notes

_____

_____

_____

Climate Map

When you study a map, read the map's title first. The title will tell you the topic of the map. Then look closely at the map key, or legend, to understand the details shown on the map.

Some plants need warm weather to grow. If they get too cold, they might die. This map helps farmers and gardeners know what to grow where they live.

Lemons do not grow well in places where it gets very cold. California, Arizona, and Florida are great places to grow lemons. Look at the map. Why do you think these are great places to grow lemons? The climate map shows that those places do not get very cold.

Lemons and other citrus fruits do not grow well in cold climates.

Robin W/Shutterstock.com

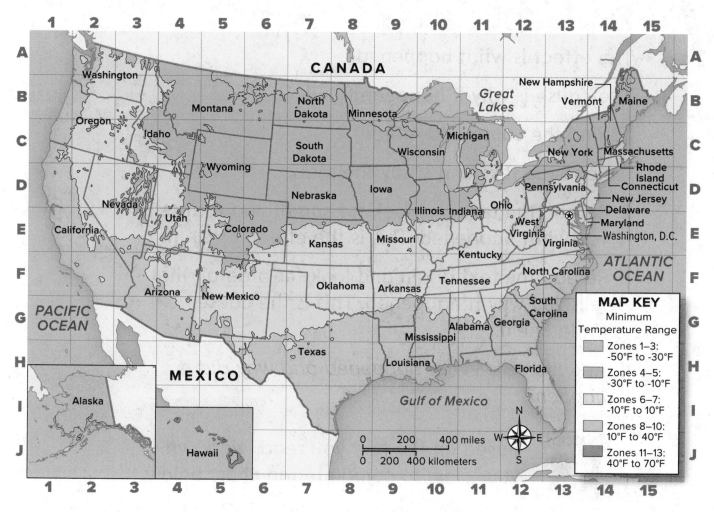

Growing zones of the United States

2 Find Evidence

Reread How does the map legend help you understand the map?

Underline details that explain who uses a climate map and why.

3 Make Connections

Talk In which climate zone do you live? Explain how to figure it out.

Explore Cause and Effect

The **effect** is what happened.

The **cause** is why it happened.

To find the cause and effect:

1. Read the text and study the map.

2. Reread the text and look for something that tells you what happened. This is the effect. Circle it.

3. Reread the text again and look for a detail that tells you why it happened. This is the cause. Underline it.

4. Ask yourself, *What happened and why did it happen?*

 COLLABORATE Based on the text you read, work with your class to complete the chart below.

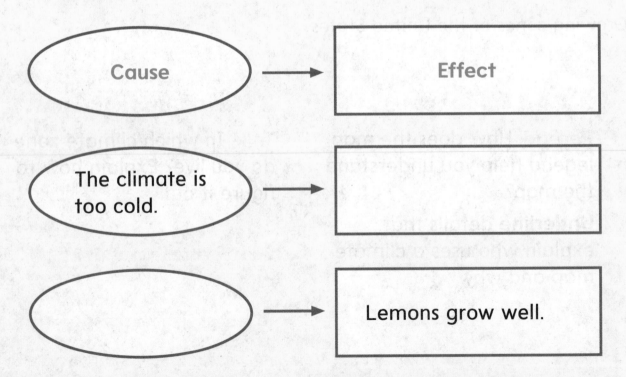

Cause	→	Effect
The climate is too cold.	→	
	→	Lemons grow well.

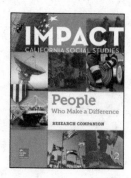

Investigate!

Read pages 172–179 in your Research Companion. Use your investigative skills to look for text evidence that tells you how climate and geography affect farming. This chart will help you organize your notes.

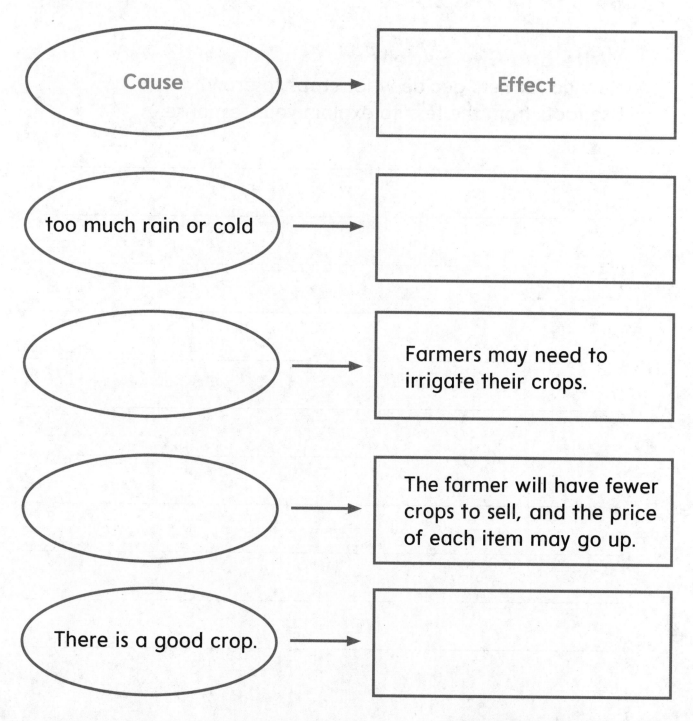

Cause	Effect
too much rain or cold	
	Farmers may need to irrigate their crops.
	The farmer will have fewer crops to sell, and the price of each item may go up.
There is a good crop.	

Think About It

Based on the information you have gathered, why do farmers need to think about geography and climate before planting crops?

Write About It

Write and Cite Evidence

How do farmers decide what crops to grow?
Use facts from the text to explain your response.

_____

_____

_____

_____

_____

_____

_____

_____

Talk About It

COLLABORATE

Explain

Share your response with a partner. Together discuss how farmers choose which plants to grow.

onomics

Connect to the EQ

ESSENTIAL QUESTION

Take Action

Choose a climate zone and create an infomercial telling people what would be the best fruits or vegetables to grow there and why. Use the space below to plan out what you will tell people.

Lesson 6

How Has Farming Changed Over Time?

Lesson Outcomes

What Am I Learning?
In this lesson, you're going to use your investigative skills to explore how farming has changed over time.

Why Am I Learning It?
Reading and talking about how farming has changed will help you learn more about the history of farming.

How Will I Know that I Learned It?
You will be able to give examples of how farming today is different from farming in the past.

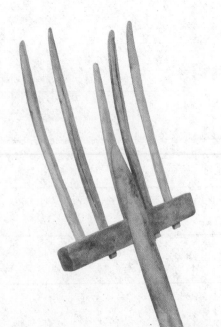

Talk About It COLLABORATE

Look closely at the picture. Was this photograph taken recently? How do you know?

(t)McGraw-Hill Education; (b)Ingram Publishing/SuperStock

Farming wheat was
very different long ago.

Working on the Farm

1 Inspect

Read Look at the caption near the painting. What does it tell you that you might not know just from looking at the painting?

Circle words you don't know.

Underline clues that tell you:

• Who is in the painting?

• What are the people doing?

• When was the painting created?

My Notes

_____

_____

_____

When you study a painting, look for a title and a date. The title of this painting is *Harvesting with Grain Cradles*. A grain cradle is a tool used to cut and gather grain. These men are using grain cradles to cut wheat. The women are gathering the wheat and tying the wheat into bundles.

We use wheat to make breads and cereals. The United States grows a lot of wheat. Working on a wheat farm was not easy long ago, and it is not easy today. Today farmers use huge machines to help with the planting and harvesting of their crops. It is still hard work to be a farmer, though.

This is what wheat farming looks like today.

Glow Images

Stanley Mazur painted *Harvesting with Grain Cradles* in about 1939.

2 Find Evidence

Reread How do captions help you understand pictures?

Underline examples of how farming has changed over time.

3 Make Connections

Talk What makes farming hard work? What work on the farm do you think would be the hardest? Explain your thinking.

Explore Compare and Contrast

When you **compare,** you tell how things are alike or similar.

When you **contrast,** you tell how things are different.

To compare and contrast:

1. Read the text all the way through and study the pictures.

2. Reread the text and look for ways the two things are alike. What do they have in common?

3. Reread the text again and look for ways the two things are different.

4. Ask yourself, *Did I find both similarities and differences?*

COLLABORATE Based on the text you read and the pictures you saw, work with your class to complete the chart.

The Past   Both   Today

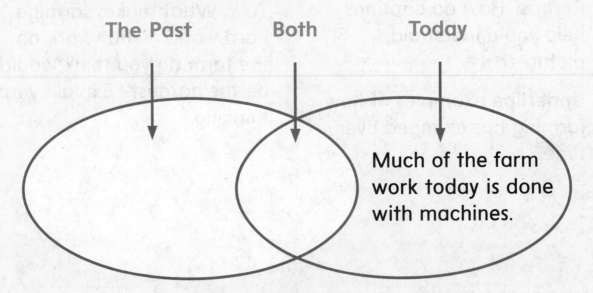

Much of the farm work today is done with machines.

Investigate!

Read pages 180–187 in your Research Companion. Use your investigative skills to look for text evidence that tells you how farming has changed over time. This chart will help you organize your notes.

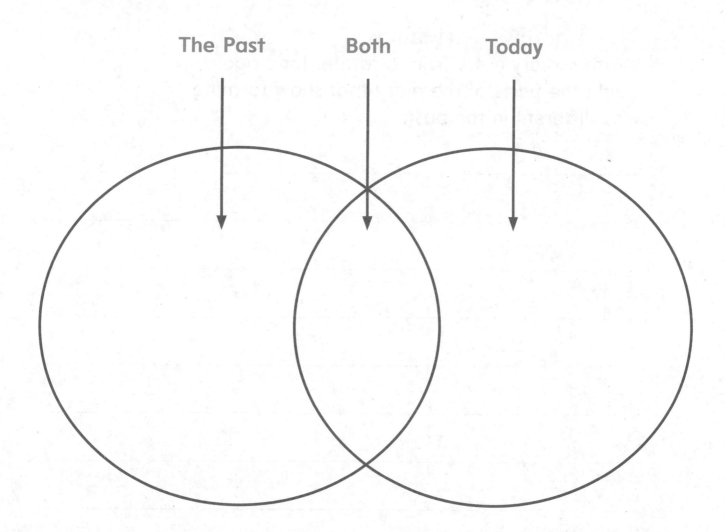

The Past   Both   Today

Think About It

Review your research. Based on the information you have gathered, how has farming changed over time?

Write About It

Write and Cite Evidence

Write a diary entry from a farmer long ago. Circle the parts of the diary that show farming was different in the past.

_____

_____

_____

_____

_____

_____

_____

_____

Talk About It

Explain

Talk with a partner about how farming is different now than it was long ago.

onomics

Connect to the

Write three reasons farming is important to all of us.

1. _____

_____

2. _____

_____

3. _____

_____

Inquiry Project Notes

_____

_____

_____

_____

From Tree to a Table!

CHARACTERS

Timber Farmer   Manufacturer

Mill Owner   Store Owner

Chorus (everyone)

Mint Images- Paul Edmondson/Mint Images RF/Getty Images

Narrator: Our story begins in a quiet forest. The timber farmer is checking the trees.

Timber Farmer: These trees take many years to grow big. I look after them to make sure they stay healthy. Some of these big ones are ready for harvest. I'd better get the cutting crew in here. My crew will bring equipment, like chainsaws, to cut the trees.

Chorus: RrrrrrRRRMM! RrrrrrRRRMM!

Timber Farmer: Here come the trucks to load the trees.

Chorus: Rumble. Rumble. Rumble.

Timber Farmer: The trucks take the timber to the local mill. The mill owner pays me for the timber.

Narrator: The timber farmer uses some of the money he earns to plant more trees. After many years, those new trees will be ready to cut. It's important to replace every tree that is cut down with a new tree to grow!

Mill Owner: I'm the mill owner. I paid the timber farmer for six loads of timber. All those tree trunks came to my sawmill on trucks.

Chorus: Vrooom! Vrooom!

Mill Owner: Sometimes they come by boat, sometimes by truck, and sometimes by train.

Chorus: Chugga chugga. Chugga chugga. Choo choo!

Mill Owner: At my sawmill, the tree trunks go through big saws.

Chorus: Buzzzzzz. Buzzzzzz.

Mill Owner: The trunks are cut into long boards, or lumber. I sell the best lumber to companies that build things. I also sell the scrap wood for other uses, like plywood or paper.

Mill Owner: I use some of the money to pay my workers. I also buy more timber to make more lumber for sale.

Manufacturer: I own a furniture factory. I buy the best lumber I can. My workers cut the lumber into parts. They put the parts together.

Chorus: Bang bang bang! Bang bang bang bang!

Manufacturer: My workers make tables, chairs, and cabinets. I sell these things to store owners. That's where most people buy their furniture. The store owner pays me.

Narrator: The manufacturer uses some of the money to pay workers. She buys more lumber to make more goods to sell. If business is good, she might hire more workers!

Store Owner: I am a store owner. I buy fine furniture, like tables, chairs, and cabinets. I put them in my stores to sell.

Chorus: Tables for sale! Chairs for sale!

(t)Onoky Photography/SuperStock; (b)McGraw-Hill Education

Store Owner: Sometimes construction companies buy my goods, too. They install cabinets for other people.

Chorus: Bang bang bang bang!

Store Owner: People buy my furniture for their homes or other buildings. Maybe you will have dinner on one of my tables.

Narrator: And that is how a tree goes from forest to table!

Inquiry Project Wrap Up

Now it is time for you to complete your flowchart and show it to your class. Here's what to do.

☐ Think about your flowchart. Do your steps make sense? Are they in order?

☐ Show your flowchart to the class.

☐ Tell your class about all the steps the food took to get to your plate.

☐ Ask your class if they understand how your food got to your plate. Answer any questions they have.

Tips for Sharing

Remember these tips when you share your flowchart with the class.

☐ Make your flowchart neat. Be sure that the steps are clear and that big arrows show how each step leads to the next.

☐ Describe each step.

☐ Speak slowly and clearly.

☐ Listen to questions your class may have.

Project Rubric

Use these questions to help evaluate your project.

	Yes	No
Did I choose one food I had for dinner?		
Did I use good sources to find out where my food came from?		
Does my flowchart look like the one that my class made together?		
Does my flowchart show the steps that the food took to get to my plate?		
Did I explain my flowchart so that my class understood it?		

Project Reflection

Think about the work that you did for the chapter project. Describe something that you think you did very well. What would you do differently next time?

_____

_____

_____

_____

Chapter 4

How Government Works

Why Do We Need Government?

In this chapter, you'll explore what government does. You'll learn about why we need government in our community, state, country, and world. You'll make a flow chart of how our government makes laws. You can also show who enforces laws and what happens when a law is broken.

Talk About It COLLABORATE

What do you wonder about government and what government does? Discuss your questions with a partner.

My Research Questions

1. _____

_____

2. _____

_____

McGraw-Hill Education

Inquiry Project

All About Laws

In this project, you'll work with a team to show how a law is made. You might also include what happens when a law is broken.

Here's your project checklist.

☐ **Write questions** about how laws are made. You will use these questions to guide your research.

☐ **Use** what you read to answer the questions. Then find more places to research if you need to.

☐ **Number** the steps in making a law in your notes. Then you will know what to put first, second, and so on.

☐ **Draw** the steps to make a flow chart. Connect the steps with arrows.

☐ **Present** your charts to the class. Explain what happens at each step.

Explore Words

Complete this chapter's Word Rater.
Write notes as you learn more about each word.

citizen   My Notes

☐ Know It!   _____

☐ Heard It!   _____

☐ Don't Know It!   _____

court   My Notes

☐ Know It!   _____

☐ Heard It!   _____

☐ Don't Know It!   _____

government   My Notes

☐ Know It!   _____

☐ Heard It!   _____

☐ Don't Know It!   _____

jury   My Notes

☐ Know It!   _____

☐ Heard It!   _____

☐ Don't Know It!   _____

law

My Notes

☐ Know It!

☐ Heard It!

☐ Don't Know It!

_____

_____

_____

nation

My Notes

☐ Know It!

☐ Heard It!

☐ Don't Know It!

_____

_____

_____

rule

My Notes

☐ Know It!

☐ Heard It!

☐ Don't Know It!

_____

_____

_____

trial

My Notes

☐ Know It!

☐ Heard It!

☐ Don't Know It!

_____

_____

_____

Why Do We Have Rules?

Lesson Outcomes

What Am I Learning?

In this lesson, you're going to use your investigative skills to explore rules.

Why Am I Learning It?

Reading and talking about rules can help us to better understand why we have them.

How Will I Know That I Learned It?

You will be able to write about rules and explain why we have them.

Talk About It

Look closely at the picture. What school rule do you think the children are following?

HSS.2.3

Following rules
helps keep us safe.

1 Inspect

Read Look at the title. What do you think this chart shows?

Circle words you don't know.

Underline the rules that the author writes about.

My Notes

_____

_____

_____

_____

_____

_____

_____

Rules

Rules are made to keep us safe. A **rule** is a guide we agree to follow. Rules help us to get along with each other. They also help to keep things fair. Fair means right for everyone.

Think about your classroom rules. What do they do? They keep everyone safe and keep work spaces clean. They help to make your classroom a better place.

When you do not follow rules in the classroom, what happens? There may be consequences. A consequence is something that happens if you do not follow a rule. It may be that you have something like recess taken away. It might be that you have to do extra work.

Look at the chart. Work with your class to fill it in. Think about your classroom rules and consequences to help you.

Our Class Rules

Classroom Rule	Reason we have this rule:	What would happen if students did not follow this rule?
1. Raise your hand and wait to be called on before speaking out.	This rule helps everyone get a chance to speak in class.	_____ _____ _____ _____
2. Keep hands, feet, and objects to yourself.	This rule helps keep students safe.	_____ _____ _____ _____
3. Walk in the classroom and school building. Do not run!	This rule helps keep students, teachers, and visitors safe.	_____ _____ _____ _____

2 Find Evidence

Reread How do the pictures help you understand the rules?

Underline the rules and circle the consequences.

3 Make Connections

Talk What did you learn about rules? Which rules do you follow in your classroom? What happens when you don't follow rules?

Explore Cause and Effect

A person, thing, or event that makes something happen is a **cause**.

The thing that actually happens because of the cause is the **effect**.

To find cause and effect:

1. Read the text once all the way through.

2. Reread the text and look for something that tells you what happened. This is the effect. Circle it.

3. Reread the text again and look for a detail that tells you why it happened. This is the cause. Underline it.

4. Ask yourself, *Did the cause lead to what happened?*

COLLABORATE Based on the text you read, work with your class to complete the chart.

Cause		Effect
I follow rules.	→	
	→	There are consequences.

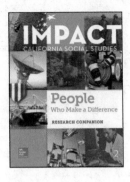

Investigate!

Read pages 198–207 in your Research Companion. Use your investigative skills to look for text evidence that tells you about rules and their effects. This chart will help you organize your notes.

Cause	Effect
washing hands	
	keeps us safe
keeping my hands to myself	

Think About It

Review your research. Based on what you have read, think about what rules are and why we need them.

Write About It

Define

What is a rule?

_____

Write and Cite Evidence

Choose a rule that you know.
Explain why we have the rule.

_____

_____

_____

_____

_____

_____

Talk About It

Explain

Find a partner who chose a different rule.
Together, discuss what you wrote.

zenship

Connect to the

Write New Rules

Write two new rules that you think are important
to follow at home, in the classroom, or at school.
Tell whey they are important.

_____

_____

_____

_____

_____

_____

Inquiry Project Notes

_____

_____

Lesson 2

How Do We Make Laws?

Lesson Outcomes

What Am I Learning?
In this lesson, you're going to use your investigative skills to explore what laws are and how they are made.

Why Am I Learning It?
Reading and talking about laws will help you understand how our government makes laws and why we have them.

How Will I Know That I Learned It?
You will be able to explain how a law keeps you safe.

Talk About It

Look closely at the picture. What do you notice about the people in the picture?

McGraw-Hill Education

The people at this meeting decided
what the laws of our country would be.

Read Look at the title. What do you think the chart shows?

Circle words you don't know.

Underline words that tell you the name of the branch and what its job is.

My Notes

_____

_____

_____

_____

_____

_____

The United States Government

A **government** is the group of people who run a country, state, or other area. The United States has a government that makes **laws**, or rules that everyone must follow. The country's government is made up of leaders. People vote for the leaders. This is why our government is sometimes called a government "by the people."

Let's look at the different branches, or parts of government. Each branch has different jobs. Different people and groups make up each branch. The branches work together. No branch has all the power.

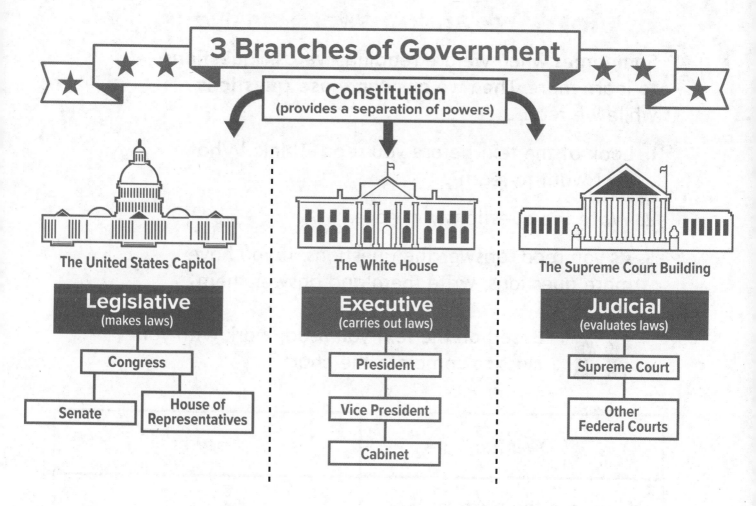

3 Branches of Government

Constitution
(provides a separation of powers)

The United States Capitol

Legislative
(makes laws)

Congress

Senate

House of Representatives

The White House

Executive
(carries out laws)

President

Vice President

Cabinet

The Supreme Court Building

Judicial
(evaluates laws)

Supreme Court

Other Federal Courts

2 Find Evidence

Reread How do the branches work in our country's government?

Circle the words in the text that tell you how people get their jobs in our government.

3 Make Connections

Talk What did you learn about government and laws? Who makes laws in our government?

Explore Ask and Answer Questions

Sometimes when we are reading, we **ask questions** to learn more. Then we **answer those questions** while we read.

1. Look at the text before you read. Think: What do I want to learn?

2. Write the questions you have.

3. As you read, answer the questions. If you have more questions, write them and answer them.

 COLLABORATE Based on the text you read, work with your class to complete the chart.

Question	Answer
What are the parts of the government?	
What does the president do?	

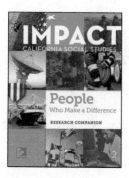

Investigate!

Read pages 208–221 in your Research Companion. Think of questions before you write. Then use your investigative skills to find the answers. This chart will help you organize your answers.

Question	Answer

Think About It

Think about your research. How do we make laws?
Who is responsible for making them?

Write About It

Define
What are laws?

_____

_____

_____

Write and Cite Evidence
Draw a picture that shows a law that keeps you
safe. Write a caption for your drawing.

```



```

Talk About It

COLLABORATE

Explain
Show your partner your work. What laws did you
draw? How do those laws keep you safe?

zenship

Connect to the EQ

ESSENTIAL
EQ
QUESTION

Make a Chart
What are the three parts in the government?
Draw a chart that shows what each part has to do
with laws.

Why Should People Follow Laws?

Lesson Outcomes

What Am I Learning?
In this lesson, you're going to use your investigative skills to explore why people should follow laws.

Why Am I Learning It?
Reading and talking about why people should follow laws will help you learn more about why laws are made.

How Will I Know that I Learned It?
You will be able to explain the consequences of not following laws.

Talk About It   COLLABORATE

Look closely at the pictures. How do they show children following a rule and a law?

How We Follow Rules and Laws

It is important to follow rules and laws to keep people safe and healthy. For example, if we let our pet off its leash, what do you think could happen? The pet could get lost or hurt. When we obey rules and laws, we show that we care about ourselves and others.

People follow laws in the community. They keep everyone safe.

Adam Gault/Digital Vision/Getty Images

People follow laws in the community. It keeps everyone safe.

2 Find Evidence

Reread Who should follow rules and laws?

Circle clues in the text and pictures that support what you think.

3 Make Connections

Talk What COLLABORATE did you learn about why we follow rules and laws?

We have rules at school and at home, and we have laws in the community, like keeping our pets on leashes. We might see people who are not following a rule or law. When this happens, we can remind them about the rule or law. Reminding someone why they should keep their pet on a leash will keep their pet safe.

If people don't follow a rule or law there is a consequence. A consequence can be small or large. It can depend on the kind of rule or law that is broken.

McGraw-Hill Education

Explore Cause and Effect

An **effect** is what happened.

A **cause** is why it happened.

To find cause and effect:

I. Read the text once all the way through.

2. Reread the text and look for something that tells you what happened. This is the effect. Circle it.

3. Reread the text again and look for a detail that tells you why it happened. This is the cause. Underline it.

4. Ask yourself, *Did the cause lead to what happened (the effect)?*

 COLLABORATE   Based on the text you read, work with your class to complete the chart.

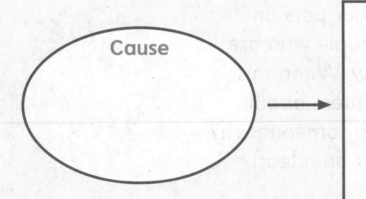

Cause

Effect

We show we care about others and ourselves.

Investigate!

Read pages 222–229 in your Research Companion. Use your investigative skills to look for text evidence that tells you about the different ways that we follow laws.

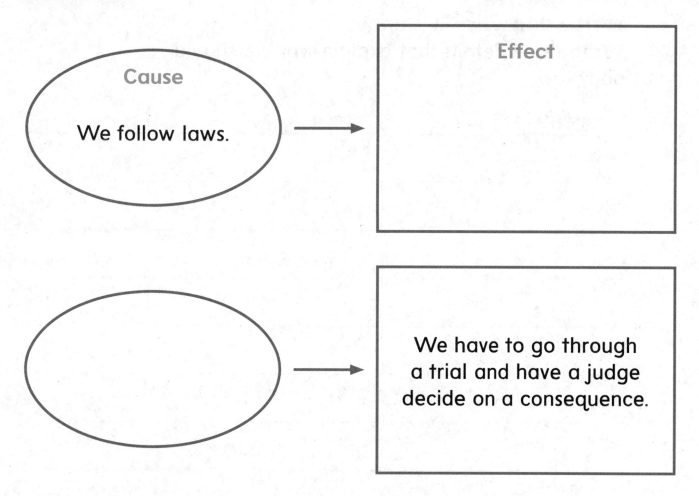

Cause

We follow laws.

Effect

We have to go through a trial and have a judge decide on a consequence.

Think About It

Review your research. Based on what you have read, think about laws and why we follow them.

Write About It

Write and Cite Evidence

Write three details that explain why we should obey laws.

_____

_____

_____

_____

_____

_____

_____

_____

_____

Talk About It

COLLABORATE

Explain

Share your response with a partner. Discuss the details you wrote about and how they affect the way you live.

zenship

Connect to the EQ

ESSENTIAL QUESTION

Take Action

Write a list of laws you might know about and what you think the consequence would be if someone broke the law.

_____

_____

_____

ESSENTIAL EQ QUESTION

Inquiry Project Notes

_____

_____

_____

_____

Lesson Outcomes

What Am I Learning?

In this lesson, you're going to use your investigative skills to explore how California's state government works.

Why Am I Learning It?

Reading and talking about how California's government works will help you learn more about what government does.

How Will I Know that I Learned It?

You will be able to explain what the California government does for the people who live here.

Talk About It

COLLABORATE

Look closely at the image of the California Constitution. How does it look like the United States Constitution on page 211 of your Research Companion?

CONSTITUTION

of the

STATE of CALIFORNIA.

We the People of California, grateful to Almighty God for our freedom, in order to secure its blessings, do establish this Constitution.

Article I.

Declaration of Rights.

Section 1.

All men are by nature free and independent, and have certain inalienable rights, among which are those of enjoying and defending life and liberty; acquiring, possessing, and protecting property; and pursuing and obtaining safety and happiness.

Sec. 2.

All political power is inherent in the people. Government is instituted for the protection, security, and benefit of the people; and they have the right to alter or reform the same, whenever the public good may require it.

Sec. 3.

The right of trial by jury shall be secured to all, and remain inviolate forever; but a jury trial may be waived by the parties, in all civil cases, in the manner to be prescribed by law.

Sec. 4.

The free exercise and enjoyment of religious profession and worship, without discrimination or preference, shall forever be allowed in this state; and no person shall be rendered incompetent to be a witness on account of his opinions on matters of religious belief; but the liberty of conscience hereby secured, shall not be so construed, as to excuse acts of licentiousness, or justify practices inconsistent with the peace or safety of this state.

Sec. 5.

The privilege of the writ of habeas corpus shall not be suspended, unless when, in cases of rebellion or invasion, the public safety may require its suspension.

Sec. 6.

Excessive bail shall not be required, nor excessive fines imposed, nor shall cruel or unusual punishments be inflicted, nor shall witnesses be unreasonably detained.

The California Constitution

1 Inspect

Read Look at the chart. What does it show?

Circle words you don't know.

Underline words that tell about laws.

My Notes

_____

_____

_____

_____

_____

_____

_____

_____

_____

California State Government

You have learned about the United States government. California also has a government. It has three parts, just like the United States government. Each part has different responsibilities. These are duties or jobs.

California's lawmakers make ideas for laws, or bills. The governor of California is the leader. The governor carries out the laws of the state.

California's judges have trials to decide if someone has broken a law. If someone has broken a law, the judges decide on a fair consequence, or punishment.

United States Government	California State Government

Makes laws for our country	Makes laws for our state
Leaders are president, lawmakers, judges	Leaders are governor, lawmakers, judges
United States citizens in all 50 states vote for leaders of our country.	United States citizens in California vote for our leaders in California.

This chart compares and contrasts United States government and the California state government.

(l)pbakerp/iStock/Getty Images; (r)YangYin/E+/Getty Images

2 Find Evidence

Reread What are responsibilities of government?

Underline clues in the text that support what you think.

3 Make Connections

Talk What did you learn about California's government?

COLLABORATE

Explore Compare and Contrast

When you **compare**, you look for ways things are alike.

When you **contrast**, you look for ways things are different.

To compare and contrast:

1. Read the text once all the way through.

2. Reread the text and look for two things that you can compare. Circle the text that shows how they are alike.

3. Reread the text again and look for how those things are different. Underline what you find.

4. Ask yourself, *How are the two things alike and different?*

COLLABORATE

Based on the text you read, work with your class to compare one thing that is alike about the two things listed in the diagram below.

California Government   United States Government

Makes laws for the state. Leaders are governor, lawmakers, judges.

Makes laws for the country. Leaders are president, lawmakers, judges.

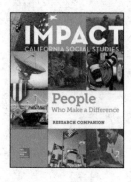

Investigate!

Read pages 230–235 in your Research Companion. Use your investigative skills to look for text evidence that tells you how California and United States governments are alike and different.

California
Government

United States
Government

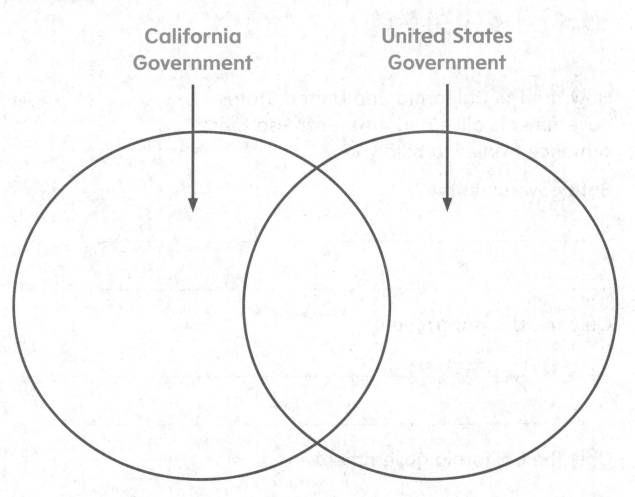

Think About It

Based on your research, think about how California state government works. Think about how it is alike and different from the United States government.

Write About It

Write and Cite Evidence

How are the California and United States governments alike and different? Use these sentence frames to help you.

Both governments

_____

_____

Only the U.S. government

_____

_____

Only the California government

_____

_____

Talk About It

Explain

Share what you wrote with a partner. Together discuss how the California state government works and how it is alike and different from the United States government.

enship

Connect to the EQ

Suppose someone asks you, "What does the California government do, and why do we need it?" Use what you have learned to write three things our state government does.

_____

_____

_____

Inquiry Project Notes

_____

_____

_____

_____

How Do Citizens and Government Work Together?

Lesson Outcomes

What Am I Learning?
In this lesson, you're going to use your investigative skills to explore how citizens work with government to make changes.

Why Am I Learning It?
Reading and talking about how citizens make changes will help you learn more about how government works.

How Will I Know that I Learned It?
You will be able to explain what citizens and government do to make communities better.

Talk About It

Look closely at the people in the picture. What kind of problems in a community could be solved by working together?

HSS.2.3.1, HSS.2.3.2

McGraw-Hill Education

Cade Martin/CDC

Citizens and government leaders can work together to solve problems.

Read Look at the title. What do you think this text is about?

Circle words you don't know.

Underline words that tell about how citizens and government work together.

My Notes

_____

_____

_____

_____

_____

_____

_____

Working Together

Citizens are an important part of our government. They help to choose our leaders. They vote for leaders they think can help solve, or fix, problems by making changes or laws.

There are different problems that our government has to solve. The government can get help from citizens. Citizens can tell their government about problems. Sometimes the solution means a law must be made, but sometimes just help from the community will solve the problem. They can share their ideas about how to solve the problems. Solving problems makes things better.

For example, if the community parks aren't clean or the playgrounds are broken, citizens can let people in the government know that there is a need for the parks to be cleaned up and for the playgrounds to be repaired. They can talk about a solution. They can work together so people can enjoy the park again.

Look at the picture on this page. What do you think the problem is? Here's how people could work together to solve the problem.

1. Make a list of ideas.

2. Talk about each idea to find the best one.

3. Try out the idea to see if it solves the problem.

4. Try another idea if the first idea does not solve the problem.

DenisTangneyJr/iStock/Getty Images

Explore Main Ideas and Key Details

The **main idea** tells what the text is mostly about.

A **key detail** tells more about the main idea.

To find the main idea and key details:

1. Read the text once all the way through.

2. Reread the text and look for a sentence that tells what the text is about. This is the main idea. Underline it.

3. Reread the text again and look for sentences that tell more about the main idea. Circle them.

4. Ask yourself, *Do the details tell more about the main idea?*

COLLABORATE Based on the text you read, work with your class to find the details that support the main idea.

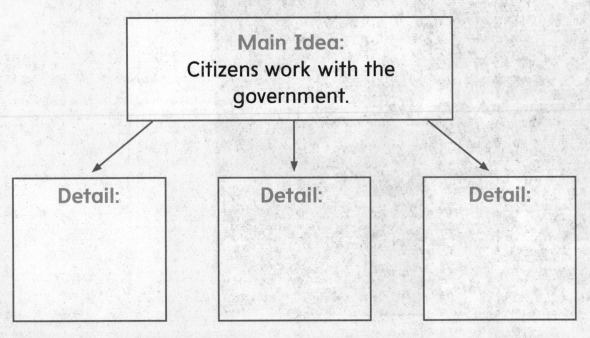

Main Idea:
Citizens work with the government.

Detail:

Detail:

Detail:

Investigate!

Read pages 236–243 in your Research Companion. Use your investigative skills to look for text evidence that tells you about how citizens work with the government.

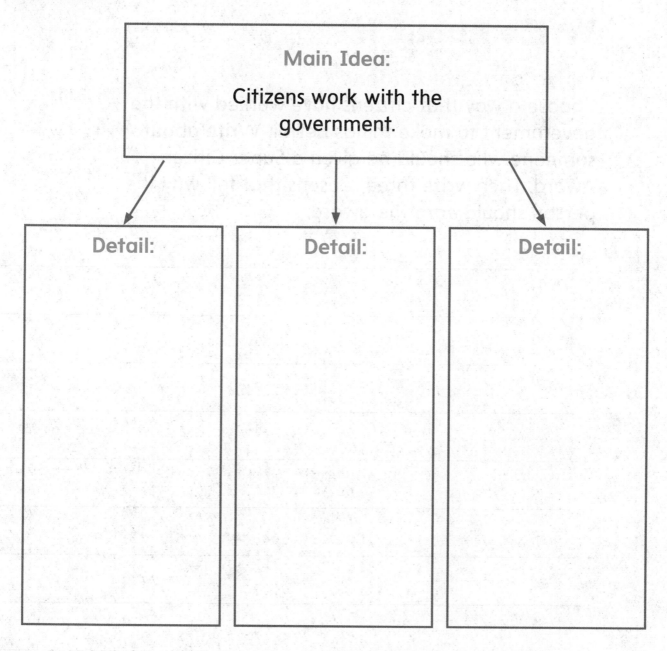

Main Idea:

Citizens work with the government.

Detail:

Detail:

Detail:

Think About It

Review your research. Based on what you have read, think about how citizens work with the government to make changes. What changes can they make?

Write About It

Write and Cite Evidence

Choose a way that citizens have worked with the government to make things better. Write about someone who should be given a Super Citizen Award. Then write three reasons that tell why the person should earn the award.

_____

_____

_____

_____

_____

_____

_____

Talk About It

COLLABORATE

Explain

Find a partner who chose the same person for the Super Citizen Award. Share what you wrote with a partner.

izenship

Connect to the EQ

ESSENTIAL QUESTION

What can you do to make your community better? Who could help you? List ideas for your plan that you could share with leaders in your community.

_____

_____

_____

_____

_____

_____

Lesson 6

How Do Countries Work Together When There Are Problems?

Lesson Outcomes

What Am I Learning?

In this lesson, you're going to use your investigative skills to explore the ways that countries work together to solve problems.

Why Am I Learning It?

Reading and talking about how countries work together to solve problems will help you learn more about how our world works today.

How Will I Know that I Learned It?

You will be able to explain what problems and solutions countries have worked on together.

Talk About It

COLLABORATE

Look closely at the picture. How do you think coming together as a group helps to solve problems?

HSS.2.3.2

McGraw-Hill Education

The United Nations is made up of countries that work together to solve problems.

Working Together in the World

1 Inspect

Read Look at the picture. What do you think this text is about?

Circle words you don't know.

Underline words that tell about how countries work together to solve problems.

My Notes

_____

_____

_____

_____

_____

_____

Citizens work with the government in their community, state, and country to solve problems. But what about problems around the world? There are bigger problems to solve. How can countries work together to solve problems?

The United Nations is a group of countries, or **nations**, around the world that work together to solve problems. The United Nations has some goals for children around the world. These goals, or things they hope to do, include:

1. All children should have a good education.

2. No child should be very poor.

3. Earth should be a clean place to live.

Digital Vision/Photodisc/Getty Images

Water polution is a problem countries have to solve together.

What kinds of world problems do you think countries have to solve? Everyone on Earth has to share the same air. If one country pollutes the air, then it is polluted for all. So many countries cooperate, or work together, to keep the air clean.

Countries also talk about keeping the water clean. Dumping garbage into the ocean can affect the whole world, not just one country. Keeping the air and water clean will help the health of the world.

2 Find Evidence

Reread Why do you think the United Nations has a goal to make Earth clean?

Underline clues in the text and pictures that support what you think.

3 Make Connections

Talk What can happen when countries cooperate?

COLLABORATE

Explore Problem and Solution

A **problem** is something you need to think about.

A **solution** is the answer to the problem.

To find the problem and solution:

1. Read the text once all the way through.

2. Reread the text and look for a sentence that talks about something that you need to think about. This is the problem. Underline it.

3. Reread the text again and look for a sentence that tells how to solve the problem. This is the solution. Circle it.

4. Ask yourself, *Does the solution solve the problem?*

COLLABORATE

Based on the text you read, work with your class to find solutions to the problem.

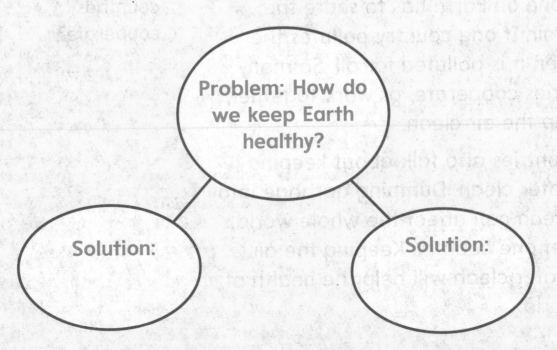

Problem: How do we keep Earth healthy?

Solution:

Solution:

Investigate!

Read pages 244-251 in your Research Companion. Use your investigative skills to look for text evidence that tells you about how countries work together to solve problems.

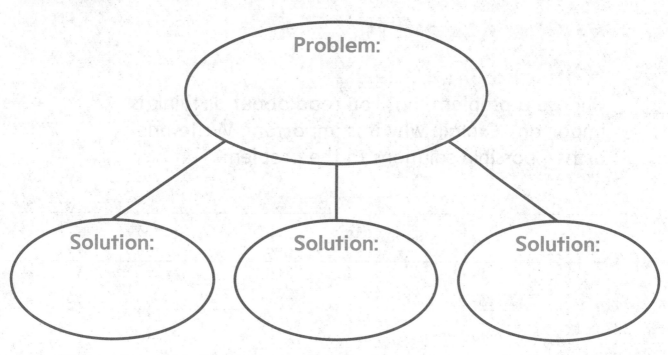

Problem:

Solution:

Solution:

Solution:

Think About It

Review your research. Based on what you have read, think about what problems countries have to solve. How do they work together with other countries to solve them?

Write About It

Write and Cite Evidence

Choose a problem that you read about or think is important. Explain why it is important. Write one or two possible solutions to the problem.

_____

_____

_____

_____

_____

_____

_____

_____

Talk About It

Explain

Find a partner who chose a different problem.
Together discuss what you wrote.

izenship

Connect to the

Write the steps that countries need to take to work
together to solve a problem.

_____

_____

_____

_____

_____

Inquiry Project Notes

_____

_____

_____

_____

_____

The Chunnel

CHARACTERS

Jacques, leader from France

Julia, leader from England

Sally, English inspector

Alain, French inspector

Cecile, French worker

Peter, English worker

John finney photography/Moment Open/Getty Images

Narrator: The year is 1988. Leaders from England and France had a meeting. They had a problem. They met to solve the problem.

Jacques: We have to find a way to work this out! There is just a thin strip of water between us. We have to find a way to make the trip between our countries faster.

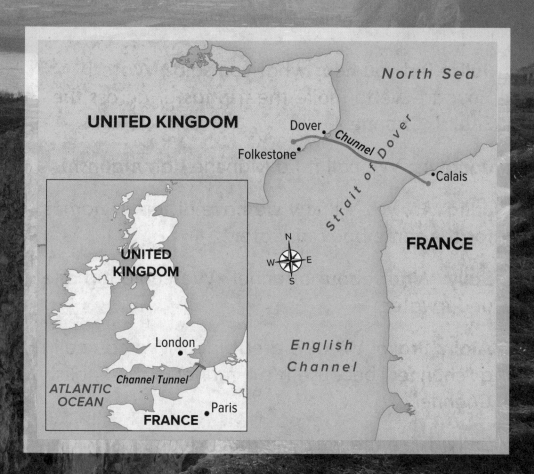

Prime Minister Thatcher of the UK and President Mitterrand of France giving the go-ahead for the Chunnel project.

Julia: Did you hear what you said? Water! How are we to make the trip faster across the English Channel?

Jacques: We call it La Manche (lah maunsh).

Julia: Ah, yes, I know we have different names for the same body of water.

Sally: What about a tunnel? We could dig one underwater.

Alain: Bravo! What a great idea! We can call it a "chunnel" because it's a *tunnel* in the English *Channel*.

Sally: I like the way you think, Alain!

Jacques: Good. Cecile, will you and your team start digging underwater from France?

Julia: Yes, and then Peter and his team will start digging underwater from England.

Peter: Will do! I look forward to meeting you in the middle, Cecile!

Cecile: Me, too! I know it will be a very long time before our meeting. Good luck!

Peter: Good luck to you, too, Cecile!

(Both teams dig for many years.)

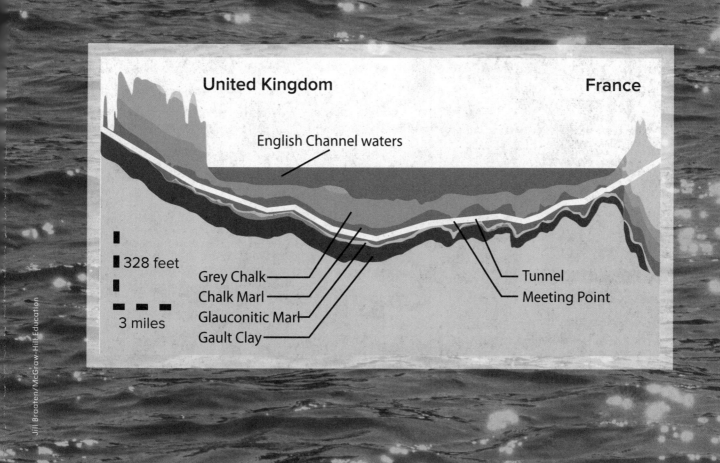

United Kingdom   France

English Channel waters

328 feet

3 miles

Grey Chalk

Chalk Marl

Glauconitic Marl

Gault Clay

Tunnel

Meeting Point

Jill Braaten/McGraw-Hill Education

Narrator: Three years later, the English team got to the meeting place. The French team was not far behind.

Peter: I wonder where Cecile could be?

Cecile: Bonjour! Here I am, Peter!

Peter: Lovely! You made it! We did it together!

qaphotos.com/Alamy Stock Photo

Alain: We have built the longest tunnel in the world! It is also the safest tunnel.

Sally: Yes, the Chunnel is the longest tunnel! It is about 30 miles long. I'm glad that we solved our problem together.

Narrator: The project to build the Chunnel was a big success. People could start using it in 1994. Now people can travel across the English Channel on passenger trains or bring their cars on special shuttle trains.

Inquiry Project Wrap Up

Now it is time for your team to share your chart with the class. Here's what to do.

☐ Show your chart to the class.

☐ Explain each part of the chart and show the steps in order.

☐ Be sure you tell about:
- how the government makes laws.
- how the government makes sure that people follow laws.
- what happens when laws are broken.

Tips for Sharing

Remember these tips when you present to your class.

☐ Look at your chart before you speak to be sure you are ready!

☐ Speak loudly, slowly, and clearly.

☐ Describe the steps in order, using words like *first, next, then,* and *when.*

☐ Answer any questions from your classmates.

Project Rubric

Use these questions to help evaluate your project.

	Yes	No
Do the charts include the steps in order?		
Are the drawings easy to understand?		
Did we explain the chart in a way that our classmates understand?		
Are all parts of the process included?		
Did we work well together as a team?		

Project Reflection

Think about the work that you did for the chapter project, either with a group or on your own. Describe something that you think you did very well. What would you do differently?

_____

_____

_____

_____

Chapter 5

People Who Make a Difference

How Can People Make a Difference in Our World?

In this chapter, you'll explore how people can make a difference in the world. You'll read about people who made the world a better place. You'll also work with a team on a chapter project to develop a plan for something that will make a difference in your school or town.

Talk About It COLLABORATE

Discuss with a partner the questions you have about people who make a difference.

My Research Questions

1. _____

_____

2. _____

_____

McGraw-Hill Education

Inquiry Project

Making a Difference in Your World

In this project, you'll work with a team to find a way to make your school or community a better place.

Here's your project checklist.

☐ **Brainstorm** some things in your school or town that you think could be better. It might be a new playground. Maybe it's a better baseball or soccer field.

☐ **Think** about each idea. Then vote on one that the team will work on.

☐ **State** your goal. What do you want to do?

☐ **Make** a poster with pictures and drawings to share your plan with others.

☐ **Present** your plan. Listen to what others have to say about your plan.

Explore Words

Complete this chapter's Word Rater.
Write notes as you learn more about each word.

boycott

☐ Know It!
☐ Heard It!
☐ Don't Know It!

My Notes

_____

_____

_____

hero

☐ Know It!
☐ Heard It!
☐ Don't Know It!

My Notes

_____

_____

_____

integrate

☐ Know It!
☐ Heard It!
☐ Don't Know It!

My Notes

_____

_____

_____

justice

☐ Know It!
☐ Heard It!
☐ Don't Know It!

My Notes

_____

_____

_____

scientist

□ Know It!
□ Heard It!
□ Don't Know It!

My Notes

_____

_____

_____

segregate

□ Know It!
□ Heard It!
□ Don't Know It!

My Notes

_____

_____

_____

What Makes a Hero?

Lesson Outcomes

What Am I Learning?

In this lesson, you're going to use your investigative skills to learn about the qualities that make a person a hero.

Why Am I Learning It?

Reading and talking about the qualities that make someone a hero will help you learn more about how people can make the world a better place.

How Will I Know that I Learned It?

You will be able to name several qualities of a hero.

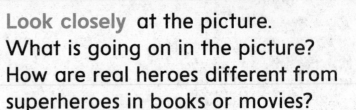

Talk About It COLLABORATE

Look closely at the picture. What is going on in the picture? How are real heroes different from superheroes in books or movies?

(t)McGraw-Hill Education; (b)Siede Preis/Photodisc/Getty Images

HSS.2.5, HAS.HR.2, HAS.HI.1

Read Look at the title. Who is the topic of this biography?

Circle words you don't know.

Underline clues that tell you:

• When did Abraham Lincoln live?

• Why do we remember Lincoln today?

• What qualities made Lincoln a hero?

My Notes

_____

_____

_____

_____

Abraham Lincoln, an American Hero

What is a hero? A **hero** is a person who does something brave or important to help others.

Abraham Lincoln was born in Kentucky in 1809. His family was not rich. He worked very hard to learn all he could. He became a soldier and then a lawyer.

Abraham Lincoln became the president of the United States in 1861. He was the president when the United States broke apart. Some states were at war with other states. This was called the Civil War. People did not know if the United States would stay as one country or become two different countries.

President Abraham Lincoln

Prints and Photographs Division, Library of Congress, LC-US262-13016

Abraham Lincoln with soldiers

President Lincoln wanted the United States to remain as one country. Lincoln led the country through the war and helped it come back together. President Lincoln is remembered for bravely saying that people who had been kept in slavery must be free. He was a hero to many people. He said that he wanted to "bind up the nation's wounds" and help the country become united again. Sadly, he was killed in 1865 before he could see that happen.

2 Find Evidence

Reread How is a biography different from a made-up story?

Draw a box around some details that are facts in the biography.

3 Make Connections

Talk Think about what made President Lincoln a hero. Turn back to page 227. What qualities do Lincoln and the firefighters have in common?

COLLABORATE

Explore Key Details

When we read, it is important to look for the **key details** that support the main idea.

Key details may tell about events, dates, facts, or the qualities of a person.

To find the key details:

1. Read the text all the way through.

2. Reread and look closely to find information that supports the main idea. Circle words that tell you more about the main idea.

3. Ask yourself, *Did I find details that tell me more about the main idea?*

COLLABORATE
Based on the text you have read, work with your class to complete the chart below.

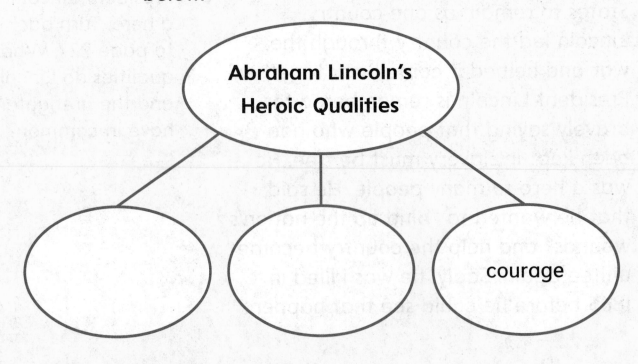

Abraham Lincoln's Heroic Qualities

courage

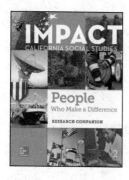

Investigate!

Read pages 262–269 in your Research Companion. Use your investigative skills to find text evidence about the qualities that make someone a hero. Make a list of the qualities and include the names of people who are examples of each quality. This chart will help you organize your notes.

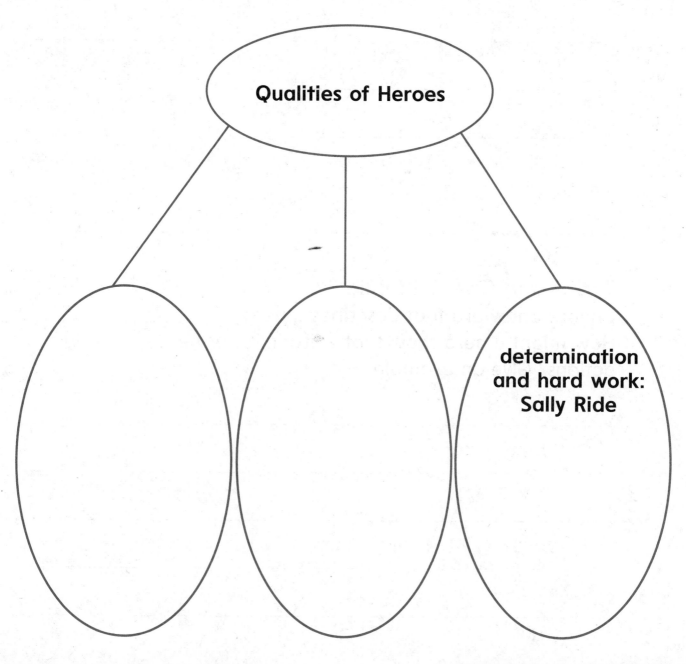

Qualities of Heroes

determination and hard work: Sally Ride

Think About It

What makes a person a hero?
What qualities do heroes have?

Write About It

Define
What is a hero?

_____

_____

_____

_____

Write and Cite Evidence
Choose one word that describes a hero.
How might a hero show that word in his or her
actions? Give an example.

_____

_____

_____

_____

Talk About It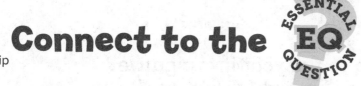

Explain

Find a partner who chose a different word.
Share what you wrote.

Connect to the EQ

Make a "Wanted" poster for a hero.
List the qualities you hope the hero will have.
Tell how the hero makes a difference.

Lesson Outcomes

What Am I Learning?

In this lesson, you're going to use your investigative skills to explore what justice is and how individuals can work for justice.

Why Am I Learning It?

Reading and talking about how individuals can work for justice will help you learn more about people who make a difference in our world.

How Will I Know that I Learned It?

You will be able to explain what justice is and describe people who have worked for justice.

> **Talk About It** COLLABORATE
>
> **Look closely** at the picture.
> Where are these people?
> When was this photo taken?
> How do you know?

Rosa Parks rides a bus after the Montgomery bus boycott in 1956.

1 Inspect

Read Look at the title. What do you think this text is about?

Circle words you don't know.

Underline the unfair laws that the author writes about.

My Notes

_____

_____

_____

_____

_____

_____

Taking a Stand

America has a tradition of working hard for freedom and **justice**, or fairness. Years ago, many states had unfair laws. The laws prevented black people from attending the same schools, eating at the same restaurants, or sitting in the same bus seats as white people. African Americans were not treated fairly.

On December 1, 1955, a woman named Rosa Parks refused to give up her bus seat to a white man. The police took her to jail.

Rosa Parks was arrested for refusing to give up her seat on the bus.

World History Archive/Alamy Stock Photo

Dr. Martin Luther King, Jr. worked with Rosa Parks. He told the people of Montgomery, Alabama, to **boycott**, or stop using, the buses until the unfair law was changed. People walked to work or school for one whole year. The bus companies lost money. Finally, the law was changed.

After the boycott, black and white people were free to sit anywhere they wanted on buses.

2 Find Evidence

Reread What kind of person do you think Rosa Parks was?

Underline clues that support what you think.

3 Make Connections

Talk What happened because of what Rosa Parks did? COLLABORATE

Turn back to page 235. Which woman do you think is Rosa Parks? Why do you think so?

Explore Cause and Effect

The **effect** is what happened.

The **cause** is why it happened.

To find cause and effect:

1. Read the text once all the way through.

2. Reread the text and look for something that tells you what happened. This is the effect. Circle it.

3. Reread the text again and look for a detail that tells you why it happened. This is the cause. Underline it.

4. Ask yourself, *Did the event lead to what happened?*

 COLLABORATE Based on the text you have read, work with your class to write the cause and effect in the chart below.

Who?	Cause	Effect
Rosa Parks		

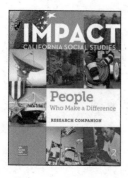

Investigate!

Read pages 270–277 in your Research Companion. Use your investigative skills to look for details that tell you what happened and why it happened. This chart will help you organize your notes.

Who?	Cause	Effect
Martin Luther King, Jr.	He told people in Montgomery to start a bus boycott.	
Malala Yousafzai		All children are able to go to school in Pakistan.
Ruby Bridges	She was a black student enrolled in an all-white school.	
Susan B. Anthony	She led marches and gave speeches about women's right to vote.	

Think About It

Review your research. Based on your research, think about how people can work for justice.

Write About It

Define
What is justice?

_____

_____

_____

Write and Cite Evidence
How can people work for justice? Use facts from the texts to explain your response.

_____

_____

_____

_____

_____

_____

Talk About It

COLLABORATE

Explain
Share your response with a partner. Together discuss how the people you researched worked for justice.

Connect to the EQ

ESSENTIAL QUESTION

Take Action
How can your class work for justice in your community? List three ideas to share with others.

1. _____

_____

_____

2. _____

_____

_____

3. _____

_____

_____

What Differences Have Scientists Made?

Lesson Outcomes

What Am I Learning?
In this lesson, you're going to use your investigative skills to learn how scientists have made differences in our lives.

Why Am I Learning It?
Reading and talking about how scientists have made differences in our lives will help you understand why scientists are heroes.

How Will I Know that I Learned It?
You will be able to name scientists and tell how they have made a difference in people's lives.

Talk About It
COLLABORATE

Look closely at the picture.
What is this scientist studying?
Where do you think he is?
How do you know?

McGraw-Hill Education

HSS.2.5, HAS.CS.3, HAS.HR.2

Painting of George Washington Carver
by Betsy Graves Reyneau, 1942

1 Inspect

Read Look at the title. Who is the topic of this text?

Circle words you don't know.

Underline clues that tell you:

- when George Washington Carver lived

- what kind of work he did

My Notes

_____

_____

_____

_____

_____

_____

George Washington Carver, Scientist

George Washington Carver was a scientist. A **scientist** studies things in nature, like animals, stars, and rocks. George Washington Carver studied plants. He wanted to help farmers grow better crops. He began teaching at a college in Alabama in 1896. He worked with farmers in the area. He studied the soil and the crops they grew. Carver made a wagon that he took from farm to farm to teach farmers. He taught them how to grow better crops.

The local farmers grew mostly cotton. Carver wanted farmers to plant more than cotton. Other plants would help the soil stay rich. He got farmers to grow peanuts. He invented new uses for peanuts. He made peanut butter. He also used peanuts to make medicines and shampoo. Sometimes farmers grew extra peanuts, and then they could sell them. They were happy to grow and sell something with so many uses.

George Washington Carver in his lab

George Washington Carver studied more than peanuts. He also found more than one hundred uses for sweet potatoes. He even used them to make candies and ink. He loved to come up with new ideas.

Carver helped farmers. He taught students. He was always interested in plants and learning all he could. George Washington Carver led an amazing life. The place where he was born was made into a national park.

2 Find Evidence

Reread What kind of person do you think George Washington Carver was?

Draw a box around clues that support what you think.

3 Make Connections

Talk Think about what George Washington Carver did. How did his learning about plants help farmers and other people?

Inquiry Tools

Explore Cause and Effect

When you read, look for causes and effects.

The **effect** is what happened. The **cause** is what made it happen.

To find cause and effect:

1. Read the text all the way through.

2. Reread and look closely to find an event that happened. Circle words that tell you about it.

3. Reread and look for a clue that helps you understand why the event happened. Underline this cause.

4. Continue to look for causes and their effects.

5. Ask yourself, *Did I find causes and effects?*

 COLLABORATE Based on the text you read, work with your class to complete the chart below.

Cause	Effect
Carver wanted farmers to grow more than cotton.	
	Farmers could sell peanuts.
Carver studied sweet potatoes.	

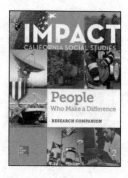

Investigate!

Read pages 278–287 in your Research Companion. Use your investigative skills to look for text evidence that tells you about causes and their effects. This chart will help you organize your notes.

Cause	Effect
Pasteur studied germs in food.	
	He invented a way to prevent polio.
	He found a way to collect and store blood.
Rachel Carson studied a pesticide called DDT.	
	He was able to have his inventions improved, and he improved the inventions of others.
Lewis Latimer improved Thomas Edison's invention.	

Think About It

Based on what you have read, how have scientists and inventions made a difference?

Write About It

Define
What is an invention?

_____

_____

_____

Write and Cite Evidence
Make a chart. List the scientists you learned about. Next to each name, write what the scientist invented or studied. Then write what effect that action had.

_____

_____

_____

_____

_____

_____

Talk About It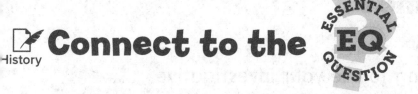

Explain

Talk with a partner about how scientists have made a difference in your life.

History

Connect to the EQ ESSENTIAL QUESTION

Choose a scientist you read about. Think of how the world would be different without the work of that scientist. Write a story about it.

_____

_____

_____

_____

_____

_____

_____

_____

_____

_____

How Do Athletes Inspire Us?

Lesson Outcomes

What Am I Learning?

In this lesson, you're going to use your investigative skills to explore athletes and what they have done to inspire others.

Why Am I Learning It?

Reading and talking about great things that athletes have done can help you better understand that people can inspire us in different ways.

How Will I Know that I Learned It?

You will be able to describe specific things athletes have done to inspire others.

Talk About It

COLLABORATE

Look closely at the picture. These athletes are getting medals at the Olympics. How do you think they feel? How can you tell?

McGraw-Hill Education

Wilma Rudolph,
gold medal winner

1 Inspect

Read Look at the title. What do you think this text is about?

Circle words you don't know.

Underline what was wrong and how it was changed.

My Notes

_____

_____

_____

_____

_____

_____

_____

Changing What's Wrong

Jackie Robinson was a great baseball player. He lived during a time when black people were not allowed to do the same things as white people. Robinson wanted to play major league baseball, but only white people were allowed to play. There was a separate baseball league for black players. He knew that was wrong and needed to change.

Jackie Robinson won the Most Valuable Player award in 1949.

Francis Miller/The LIFE Picture Collection/Getty Images

Jackie Robinson scoring the winning run, June 18, 1952

In 1947 Robinson became the first black baseball player in the major leagues. He showed great courage. Many white people did not want him to play on a major league team. Even some of his own teammates were upset.

Robinson spoke out about unfair treatment of others. He helped work for equality of all people. Robinson helped inspire other athletes. When you inspire people, you make them want to do something great.

2 Find Evidence

Reread What made Jackie Robinson inspiring?

Underline clues that support what you think.

3 Make Connections

Talk How did Jackie Robinson help to change what was wrong?

COLLABORATE

Turn back to page 251. What do Jackie Robinson and these athletes have in common?

Explore Main Idea and Details

The **main idea** tells what the text is about.

Details tell more about the main idea.

To find the main idea and details:

1. Read the text once all the way through.

2. Reread and look for something that tells you what the text is mostly about. This is the main idea. Circle it.

3. Reread the text again and look for sentences that tell more about the main idea. Those are details. Underline them.

4. Ask yourself, *Do the details support the main idea?*

COLLABORATE   Based on the text you have read, work with your class to write details in the web below.

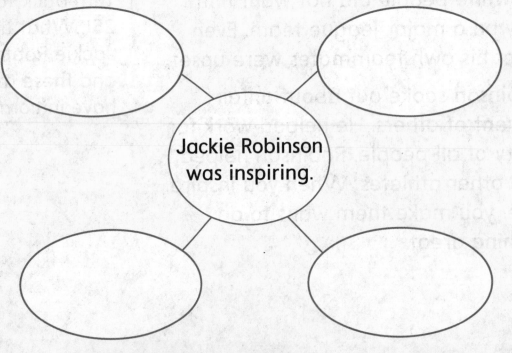

Jackie Robinson was inspiring.

Investigate!

Read pages 288–295 in your Research Companion. Use your investigative skills to find details about athletes that support the main idea. This web will help you organize your notes.

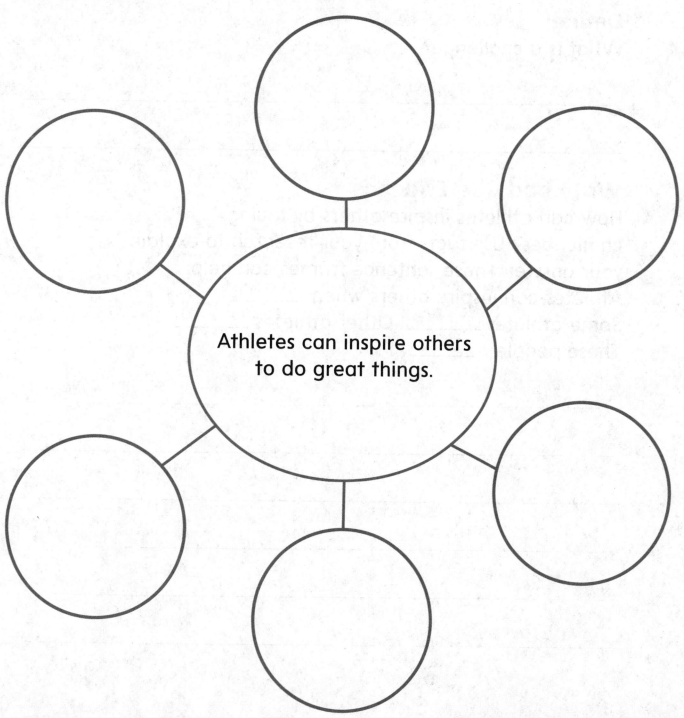

Athletes can inspire others to do great things.

Think About It

Review your research. Think about how the athletes you read about faced challenges.

Write About It

Define
What is a challenge?

_____

_____

Write and Cite Evidence
How can athletes inspire others by facing challenges? Use facts from your research to explain your answer. These sentence frames can help:

Athletes can inspire others when _____.

Some athletes _____. Other athletes _____.

These people _____.

_____

_____

_____

_____

_____

Talk About It

Explain

Explain to a partner how these athletes beat challenges and inspired others.

Connect to the EQ

Give Your Opinion

Choose one athlete that you read about. Give at least three reasons why that person inspires you.

1. _____

_____

2. _____

_____

3. _____

_____

Inquiry Project Notes

_____

_____

_____

They Made a Difference!

CHARACTERS

Narrator (teacher)
Speakers 1, 2, 3, 4, 5, and 6
Group A
Group B

Narrator: Many people make a difference! A hero can be anyone.

Speaker 1: You might not know his name—but he changed history! He made the first antibiotic from a dish full of mold. It sounds gross, but it saved lives. His medicine was called penicillin.

Group A: Who was he?

Group B: He was Sir Alexander Fleming!

Prisma Archivo/Alamy Stock Photo

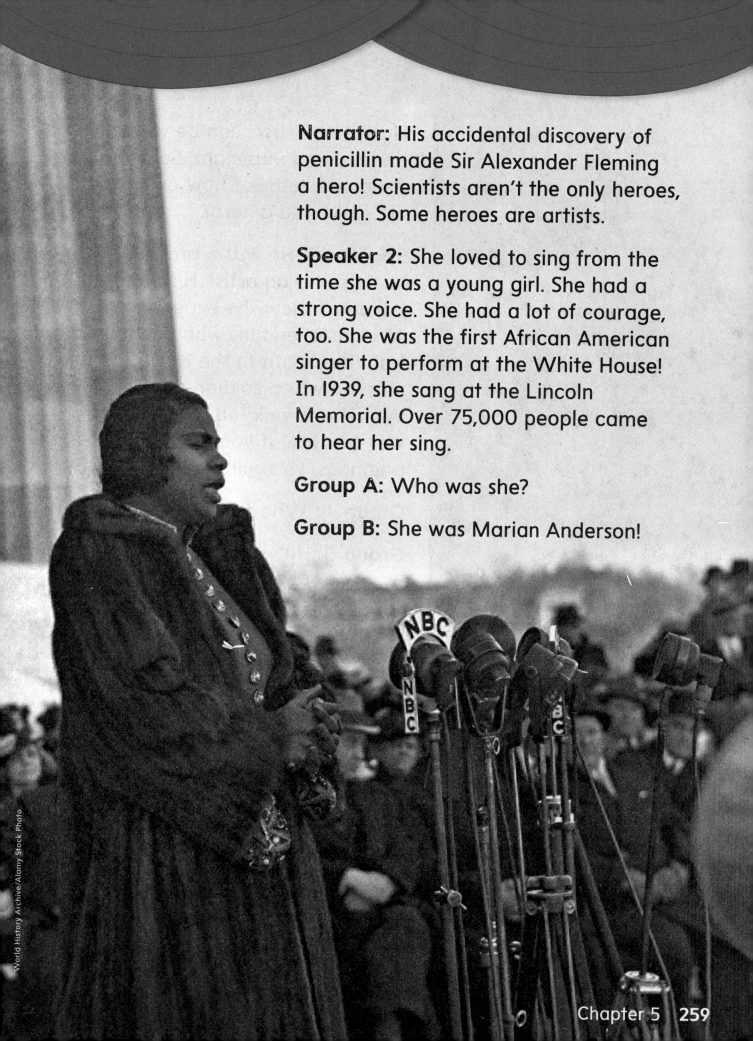

Narrator: His accidental discovery of penicillin made Sir Alexander Fleming a hero! Scientists aren't the only heroes, though. Some heroes are artists.

Speaker 2: She loved to sing from the time she was a young girl. She had a strong voice. She had a lot of courage, too. She was the first African American singer to perform at the White House! In 1939, she sang at the Lincoln Memorial. Over 75,000 people came to hear her sing.

Group A: Who was she?

Group B: She was Marian Anderson!

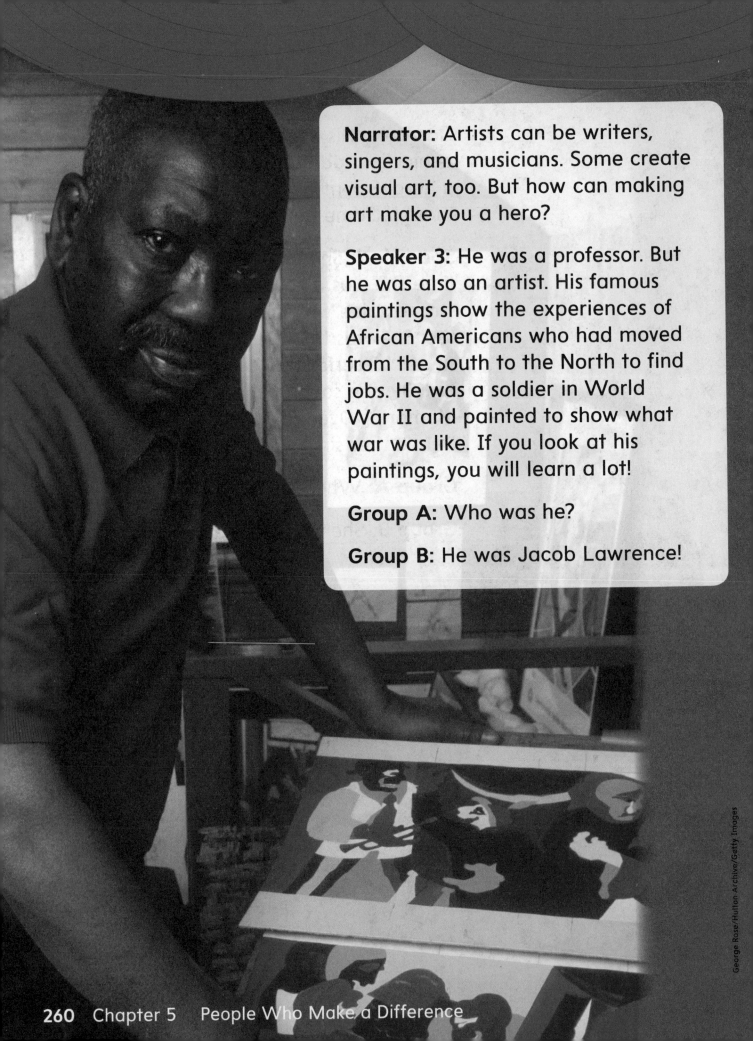

Narrator: Artists can be writers, singers, and musicians. Some create visual art, too. But how can making art make you a hero?

Speaker 3: He was a professor. But he was also an artist. His famous paintings show the experiences of African Americans who had moved from the South to the North to find jobs. He was a soldier in World War II and painted to show what war was like. If you look at his paintings, you will learn a lot!

Group A: Who was he?

Group B: He was Jacob Lawrence!

George Rose/Hulton Archive/Getty Images

Narrator: Scientists, artists...who else can be heroes? What about people just like you and me?

Speaker 4: She was a schoolgirl from Maine who wrote a letter to a leader in the Soviet Union in 1982. The leader invited her to visit. The United States and the Soviet Union weren't friends, but she decided to go anyway. She helped make peace there and in other countries around the world. She did all this before she was 13!

Group A: Who was she?

Group B: She was Samantha Reed Smith.

ITAR-TASS Photo Agency/Alamy Stock Photo

Narrator: A young person can do something really inspiring! How else can young people make a difference?

Speaker 5: She was lonely at lunch. No one would sit with her. She knew that other students felt lonely and bullied, too. She invented an app for mobile devices. You can use it to find friends to sit with at lunch or to invite others to sit with you. Now no one needs to feel lonely or sad!

Group A: Who was she?

Group B: She was Natalie Hampton.

SolStock/iStockphoto/Getty Images

Narrator: Artists, scientists, and maybe even your neighbors and friends can all be heroes! But some heroes have four legs instead of two.

Speaker 6: Some of them have pulled people from burning buildings. Some can sniff and find people who are missing. Some of them make people who are sick, worried, or sad feel better just by being close by.

Group A: Who are they?

Group B: They are hero dogs!

Narrator: Other animals can be heroes, too, not just dogs. A cat alerted a woman when her husband was in danger. Pigeons carried secret messages during a war. Dolphins have rescued lost swimmers, too!

Group A: Who's your favorite hero?

Group B: Look in the mirror! <u>Your</u> hero could be...

All: ME!!!

Inquiry Project Wrap Up

Now it is time for your team to share your project with the rest of the class. Here's what to do.

☐ Share your plan. Talk about what your goal was.

☐ Explain why your idea would make the school or community a better place.

☐ Talk about how well you think it worked. Describe what you accomplished.

☐ Show your project poster.

Tips for Presenting

Remember these tips when you present to your class.

☐ Prepare your presentation.

☐ Speak loudly and clearly.

☐ Look at your listeners and smile.

☐ Relax and enjoy yourself!

Project Rubric

Use these questions to help evaluate your project.

	Yes	No
Does our project have a goal?		
Is there a clear plan that shows what we need to do and how we will get it done?		
Did we talk to someone who could help us with our plan?		
Did our plan work out as we expected?		
Did we work well as a team?		

Project Reflection

Think about the work that you did in this chapter, either with a group or on your own. Describe something that you think you did very well. What would you do differently?

_____

_____

_____

_____

Reference Section

The Reference Section has a glossary of vocabulary words from the chapters in this book. Use this section to explore new vocabulary as you investigate and take action.

Glossary

A

absolute location The exact place where something is. The **absolute location** of my school is 25 Oak Lane.

artifact Object from the past. This tool is an **artifact** that was made a long time ago.

B

boycott To refuse to buy or use a product as a form of protest. They decided to **boycott** the restaurant and not go there until it decides to recycle its trash.

C

citizen A member of a community, state, or nation. A **citizen** has a responsibility to obey the laws.

community A place where people live, work, and have fun together. My cousin lives in the **community** of Santa Monica, California.

compass rose A symbol on a map that points to the letters N, S, E, and W. The **compass rose** helps me know that the United States is south of Canada.

consumer The person who buys and uses the goods and services sold by others. A **consumer** buys groceries at the store.

continent A very large area of land. The United States is on the **continent** of North America.

court A building where judges work. People go to **court** to get help if they can't agree about a law.

culture The way a group of people live, including their food, music, and traditions. Mariachi music is part of the Mexican **culture**.

D

distributor A person or company that supplies stores with goods to sell. The factory uses a **distributor** to get the jelly to the stores.

G

geography The study of the things that make up our Earth. I like to study **geography** to learn more about Earth.

goods The things we buy. We buy **goods** like markers and paper at the store.

government A group of people who run a community, state, or country. Mayors are part of the **government** in many communities.

H

hero A person who does something brave or important to help others. Teachers, firefighters, and police officers are **heroes** in our community.

history The story of what happened in the past. You can learn about your town's **history** from photographs.

I

immigrant A person who comes to live in a country that is new to them. My great grandfather was an **immigrant** from Germany.

integrate To come together. People worked to **integrate** the schools so children of all backgrounds could learn together.

J

jury A group of citizens who are chosen to listen to a trial and work with the judge to decide what is fair. My dad was chosen to be on a **jury**.

justice To judge fairly. We want **justice** and respect for all people.

L

law A rule for a community or government. We follow the **law** that tells us to wear our seatbelts in the cars.

location The place where something is. The **location** of the office is near the front of the school.

N

nation An area of land that is controlled by its own government. We live in the **nation** of the United States of America.

needs Things people must have to live. Food, shelter, and clothing are **needs**.

P

past The time before now. My mother lived in Oregon in the **past**.

present Today or the time we are living in now. I think we are lucky to live in the **present** because we have computers now.

primary source A source made or used by people during the time you are studying. This letter written by a pioneer long ago is a **primary source**.

processor The person or company that prepares or makes a product. The **processor** of the jelly is located in Oregon.

producer Someone who makes or grows products, or goods, to sell. A farmer is a **producer** who grows food.

protest To show that you do not agree with something. The farm workers joined together to **protest** the poor working conditions.

R

relative location Where a place is compared to another place. The **relative location** of the park is across from the school.

rural A community with few buildings away from a city. I went to visit my grandma's farm in a **rural** community.

rule A guide we agree to follow. One **rule** of the game is to take turns.

S

scarcity When there is not enough of something. There is a **scarcity** of the most popular toy because everybody wants one.

scientist A person who studies and works in a special part of science. A **scientist** is working to find a way to use seawater for fuel.

secondary source A source created later by people who studied the events or time, but who did not experience them. This new book about the explorers is a **secondary source**.

segregate To keep separate. The school once tried to **segregate** the students by their race.

services Useful things people do for others. Nurse and plumbers perform **services** that help us when we need it.

suburban A community with some homes and businesses near a city. I was born in a **suburban** community near Los Angeles.

tradition A special way of doing something that is passed down over time. Wearing a special outfit for the holiday is a **tradition** in my family.

trial A meeting to decide if someone broke a law. The judge listens to both sides during a **trial**.

urban The area of a city. Los Angeles is a large **urban** community with many tall buildings.

wants Things that people would like to have but do not need. Toys, games, and fancy shoes are **wants**.

California HSS Standards

Grade Two
Historical and Social Sciences
Content Standards and Analysis Skills

History-Social Sciences Content Standards.

People Who Make a Difference

Students in grade two explore the lives of actual people who make a difference in their everyday lives and learn the stories of extraordinary people from history whose achievements have touched them, directly or indirectly. The study of contemporary people who supply goods and services aids in understanding the complex interdependence in our free-market system.

2.1 Students differentiate between things that happened long ago and things that happened yesterday.

1. Trace the history of a family through the use of primary and secondary sources, including artfacts, photographs, interviews, and documents.
2. Compare and contrast their daily lives with those of their parents, grandparents, and/or guardians.
3. Place important events in their lives in the order in which they occurred (e.g., on a time line or storyboard).

2.2 Students demonstrate map skills by describing the absolute and relative locations of people, places, and environments.

1. Locate on a simple letter-number grid system the specific locations and geographic features in their neighborhood or community (e.g., map of the classroom, the school).
2. Label from memory a simple map of the North American continent, including the countries, oceans, Great Lakes, major rivers, and mountain ranges. Identify the essential map elements: title, legend, directional indicator, scale, and date.
3. Locate on a map where their ancestors live(d), telling when the family moved to the local community and how and why they made the trip.
4. Compare and contrast basic land use in urban, suburban, and rural environments in California.

2.3 Students explain governmental institutions and practices in the United States and other countries.

1. Explain how the United States and other countries make laws, carry out laws, determine whether laws have been violated, and punish wrongdoers.
2. Describe the ways in which groups and nations interact with one another to try to resolve problems in such areas as trade, cultural contacts, treaties, diplomacy, and military force.

2.4 Students understand basic economic concepts and their individual roles in the economy and demonstrate basic economic reasoning skills.

1. Describe food production and consumption long ago and today, including the roles of farmers, processors, distributors, weather, and land and water resources.
2. Understand the role and interdependence of buyers (consumers) and sellers (producers) of goods and services.
3. Understand how limits on resources affect production and consumption (what to produce and what to consume).

2.5 Students understand the importance of individual action and character and explain how heroes from long ago and the recent past have made a difference in others' lives (e.g., from biographies of Abraham Lincoln, Louis Pasteur, Sitting Bull, George Washington Carver, Marie Curie, Albert Einstein, Golda Meir, Jackie Robinson, Sally Ride).

Historical and Social Sciences Analysis Skills

In addition to the standards, students demonstrate the following intellectual, reasoning, reflection, and research skills:

Chronological and Spatial Thinking

1. Students place key events and people of the historical era they are studying in a chronological sequence and within a spatial context; they interpret time lines.
2. Students correctly apply terms related to time, including *past, present, future, decade, century,* and *generation.*
3. Students explain how the present is connected to the past, identifying both similarities and differences between the two, and how some things change over time and some things stay the same.
4. Students use map and globe skills to determine the absolute locations of places and interpret information available through a map's or globe's legend, scale, and symbolic representations.
5. Students judge the significance of the relative location of a place (e.g., proximity to a harbor, on trade routes) and analyze how relative advantages or disadvantages can change over time.

Research, Evidence, and Point of View

1. Students differentiate between primary and secondary sources.
2. Students pose relevant questions about events they encounter in historical documents, eyewitness accounts, oral histories, letters, diaries, artifacts, photographs, maps, artworks, and architecture.
3. Students distinguish fact from fiction by comparing documentary sources on historical figures and events with fictionalized characters and events.

Historical Interpretation

1. Students summarize the key events of the era they are studying and explain the historical contexts of those events.
2. Students identify the human and physical characteristics of the places they are studying and explain how those features form the unique character of those places.
3. Students identify and interpret the multiple causes and effects of historical events.
4. Students conduct cost-benefit analyses of historical and current events.